THE SINFUL MATERNAL

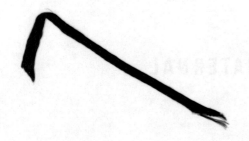

Bernadette Marie Calafell, Marina Levina,
and Kendall R. Phillips, General Editors

The

SINFUL
MATERNAL

*Motherhood in
Possession Films*

Lauren Rocha

UNIVERSITY PRESS OF MISSISSIPPI / JACKSON

The University Press of Mississippi is the scholarly publishing agency of
the Mississippi Institutions of Higher Learning: Alcorn State University,
Delta State University, Jackson State University, Mississippi State University,
Mississippi University for Women, Mississippi Valley State University,
University of Mississippi, and University of Southern Mississippi.

www.upress.state.ms.us

The University Press of Mississippi is a member
of the Association of University Presses.

Library of Congress Cataloging-in-Publication Data

Names: Rocha, Lauren, author.
Title: The sinful maternal : motherhood in possession films / Lauren Rocha.
Other titles: Horror and monstrosity studies series.
Description: Jackson : University Press of Mississippi, 2024. | Series:
Horror and monstrosity studies series | Includes bibliographical
references and index.
Identifiers: LCCN 2023054137 (print) | LCCN 2023054138 (ebook) | ISBN
9781496851734 (hardback) | ISBN 9781496851741 (trade paperback) | ISBN
9781496851758 (epub) | ISBN 9781496851765 (epub) | ISBN 9781496851772
(pdf) | ISBN 9781496851789 (pdf)
Subjects: LCSH: Horror films—History and criticism. | Motherhood in motion
pictures. | Mothers in motion pictures. | BISAC: PERFORMING ARTS / Film
/ History & Criticism | SOCIAL SCIENCE / Popular Culture
Classification: LCC PN1995.9.H6 R623 2024 (print) | LCC PN1995.9.H6
(ebook) | DDC 791.43/65252—dc23/eng/20240108
LC record available at https://lccn.loc.gov/2023054137
LC ebook record available at https://lccn.loc.gov/2023054138

British Library Cataloging-in-Publication Data available

CONTENTS

ACKNOWLEDGMENTS

I would like to express my deepest appreciation to those who helped me in the writing and publishing process. This book would not be possible without the support, enthusiasm, and guidance from my editor, Emily Snyder Bandy, along with Michael Martella, Valerie Jones, Amy Atwood, Joey Brown, the rest of the team at the University Press of Mississippi, and Laura J. Vollmer.

Parts of this book emerged from presentations at the Popular Culture Association/American Association national conferences. I am grateful to the friends I've made over the years at this conference who listened, provided feedback and advice, and furthered my love of the paranormal. I owe a debt of gratitude to the folks along the way who nurtured this interest, including John Kucich, Ann Brunjes, Kimberly Chabot Davis, and Ellen Scheible from Bridgewater State University and Brigitte Bailey, Christina Ortmeier-Hooper, Samantha Katz Seal, and David Waters from the University of New Hampshire, along with Leah Williams. Special thanks to my colleagues at Merrimack College whose conversations about women and horror inspired some of the ideas in this book, including Lyena Chavez, Cinzia DiGiulio, Luis Saenz De Viguera, Ellen McWhorter, Debra Michals, and Brandi Baldock.

I was inspired by the mothers and mother figures in my life when writing this. I also found myself reflecting on my own motherhood and the support network I have as my family. I give heartfelt thanks to Maxwell Becker, who watched and rewatched every film in this book, respected the space needed to research and write, and officially became a fellow lover of horror in the process.

THE SINFUL MATERNAL

It Comes from Inside
Horror, Home, and Possession

The horror genre draws from many of our deepest fears in creating narratives meant to shock, terrify, and disturb us. A loved one taken over by a nonhuman, or supernatural, entity is among those fears. Possession films encapsulate this and often target characters who are the most vulnerable, such as pregnant women, mothers, and children. While possession is typically thought to be caused by a demonic entity, the possessed body can be one inhabited by other creatures as well. The commonality is that whatever shares the skin of a character morphs the body and self into one that reveals dark desires and sinful thoughts.

Possession films often feature a woman possessed by a seemingly masculine presence. Tanya Krzywinksa explains the traditional portrayal of possessed women in horror:

> These films centre possession around the hysterical female body: the exorcists are all men and they are frequently "fathers" (of the priestly kind) with all the symbolic connotations of patriarchy. This suggests that the anarchy of possession can be read as a challenge to their hegemonic rule. . . . Over the bodies and desires of cloistered women these men play out fantasies of defeating the "bad" demonic father in the name of the "good" heavenly father. (253)

She characterizes the possession by a male demon as "symptomatic of the precarious nature of masculine identity" by putting "into question the gendered status of the male protagonists" (Krzywinksa 248). Women's bodies, Krzywinska argues, function as the site of possession in order to combat the notion of unstable masculine identity (248). The masculine is often contested in possession films; however, possessed women's bodies can also function to represent challenges to identity and the maternal role in the home.

The spectacle of possession is framed in the performativity of gender, which "revolves around . . . the way in which the anticipation of a gendered essence produces that which it posits as outside itself. . . . [P]erformativity is not a singular act, but a repetition and a ritual, which achieves its effects through its naturalization in the context of a body" (Butler xv). Performativity of gender lends itself to the narrower performativity of motherhood, a concept embedded throughout my research that focuses on the portrayal of mothers and their enacting of certain gendered, maternal characteristics. In *Men, Women, and Chainsaws*, Carol J. Clover writes:

> The female body at the center of the possession story is the object of concern not because it is missing something, but because it seems to have got, in a sense, something extra. The occult genre in general is remarkably uninterested in castration and remarkably interested in female insides—in the workings of menstruation and pregnancy, in whether and how those functions, and the female insides in general, might feel. Possession films thus take on the "occult" in its original sense (that which is hidden, derived from the Latin *occultus*, past principal of *occulere*, "conceal"), a sense that in turn squares nicely with Freud's notion of uncanny sensations as the effect of the "former *Heim* [home] of all human beings." They are exactly about what cannot be seen—not nonexistent and not even precisely unseeable, but hidden: the inner life. So the occult film's preoccupation with evidence, signs, proof; these attest to the reality of that which is obscured from view. (109)

The possession in such films is often questioned in regard to whether or not it is, in fact, supernatural or whether it can be explained by other causes. Doctors and others in the medical field are turned to in hopes that it is something that can be treated and, therefore, controlled. Just as in real life, however, the medical field often exacerbates the problem by dismissing women's fears over the body. Even worse, the medical field can normalize these fears so that women end up trapped by both the human and nonhuman.

At its heart, this book is about the relationships between mothers and motherhood. Pregnancy, birth, and the postpartum period are difficult phases whose impact on women's physical, mental, and emotional health has been historically minimized, ignored, and neglected. Simply put, a mother's body is not her own. It is a public body that is shared by her partner, children, and those around her. This shared-body motif continues to be alive today with the Supreme Court decision to overturn *Roe v. Wade* and the contested battle over access to the abortion pill. These judicial matters further limit women to their sexual and reproductive states rather than see them as individuals entitled to bodily autonomy. Women, in short, are always possessed by unseen forces that forcibly seek to control and restrict them in accordance with patriarchal laws.

Yet, if a woman does become pregnant, she is marked as sinful by the nature of the act of reproduction; she is more sinful if she thinks about terminating the pregnancy. The only way to atone for such sin, according to the patriarchal powerheads, is to become a mother and raise the child. Anything else is seen as monstrous, unholy, and that which needs to be punished under penalty of law. Even once a mother, a woman is still damned: damned to forever face the disapproval of the critics.

What does it mean, then, for a mother to be possessed? Chaos. An internal tearing open of the self. An act that, in doing so, upsets and fascinates the family who must then reorganize the exposed and stitch up that which is revealed or face its rebellious, revolting power.

Of course, sometimes, it is not the mother who is possessed. Sometimes, the child is the one under the control of a nonhuman entity. Still, even if another is possessed instead of the mother, the mother is still part of the possession. As the procreative epicenter of the family, she always possesses the inherited roles of creator, nurturer, and destroyer. Because her body is never truly her own, possession of another member of the family inherently means her own possession. This is especially true in the case of the possessed child. A symbol of the family legacy and fulfillment of the mother's duty as creator, a child, when possessed, threatens to rip apart the bastion of traditional family values in face of a corrosive, ruinous power.

A mother who becomes possessed morphs from the nurturing creator to the terrifying destroyer. Because the mother is implicitly linked to the possession of the child through her maternal, creator role, she becomes that which must be feared. Julia Kristeva notes, "Fear of the archaic mother turns out to be essentially fear of her generative power. It is this power, a dreaded one, that patrilineal filiation has the burden of subduing. It is thus not surprising to see pollution rituals proliferating in societies where patrilineal power is poorly secured, as if the latter sought, by means of purification, a support against excessive matrilineality" (77). Possession of the child can be seen as such an excess since the child can be read as a doppelganger of the parent. Sigmund Freud outlines the concept of the doppelganger by saying that a doppelganger has "the appearance of persons who have to be regarded as identical because they look alike. This relationship is intensified by the spontaneous transmission of mental processes from one of these persons to the other—what we would call telepathy—so that one becomes the co-owner of the other's knowledge, emotions and experiences" (141). The child acts as the parent's doppelganger through "the constant recurrence of the same thing, the repetition of the same facial features, the same characters, the same destinies, the same misdeeds, even the same names, through successive generations" and the substitution of the doppelganger's self for that of the original individual (Freud 141–42). Since the child's body is one that emerged from the mother's body, their deviant behavior when possessed is inherently tied to the mother's own failings.

Even if the mother is not physically present in these narratives, the abstract mother—that is, the archaic mother—is. Barbara Creed writes:

> The archaic mother is present in all horror films as the blackness of extinction—death. The desires and fears invoked by the image of the archaic mother, as a force that threatens to reincorporate what it once gave birth to, are always there in the horror text—all pervasive, all encompassing—because of the constant presence of death. The desire to return to the original oneness of things, to return to the mother/womb, is primarily a desire for non-differentiation. (28)

The possessed body can therefore be read as a maternal body. In threatening to completely take over a character's body, a possessing entity brings with it the threat of procreative metamorphosis that can invert the mother into one that undermines the patriarchal order through embracing the darkness of the inside.

The possessed body is one that is abject, "related to perversion. . . . The abject is perverse because it neither gives up nor assumes a prohibition, a rule, or a law; but turns them aside, misleads, corrupts; uses them, takes advantage of them, the better to deny them" (Kristeva 15). Jeffrey Jerome Cohen applies Kristeva's theory of the abject to the monstrous, remarking, "The monster is an incorporation of the Outside, and the Beyond. . . . Any kind of alterity can be inscribed across (constructed through) the monstrous body" (7). As a result, possession calls into question and ultimately reshapes an individual's internal identity through the harsh treatment of their physical bodies as "the body's inside . . . [that] shows up in order to compensate for the collapse of the border between inside and outside. It is as if the skin, a fragile container, no longer guaranteed the integrity of one's 'own and clean self' but, scraped or transparent, invisible or taut, gave way before the dejection of its contents" (Kristeva 53). Characters who are possessed are often shown expelling bodily fluids, adding to the body's abject state because "urine, blood, sperm, excrement then show up in order to reassure a subject that is lacking its 'own and clean self'" (Kristeva 53). The possessed body defies categorization and marks itself as monstrous in its resistance to order and structure. The possessed body is chaos that threatens to spread beyond its corporeal container, the contained turned uncontrollable.

Possession films are films with mother issues. Whether the target of possession or bystanders to the possession of a loved one, women are intricately connected to the supernatural. Women have complemented and been complicit with the devil throughout history. We have been objectified, marginalized, and demonized in countless narratives and are still today. The patriarchy is right to fear the possessed woman for her chaos is one that can rip apart their power.

The House That Haunts[1]

Aiding in the possession narrative, the house stands as a symbol of the façade of stability. When the family is unstable, the house can be looked at as a form of stability and structure. The problem, of course, is that whatever issues a family had before moving in continue once their address changes. As the films in this book highlight, the house can serve to exacerbate familial tensions through its own strife-ridden structure.

Homes become transformed into sites ripe to upset domestic stability through possession, putting relationships between mothers and their children into question as maternal authority is challenged by an invasive supernatural presence. The monster in these films appears during times of domestic discord, heightening tensions to demonstrate the fragility of familial constructs. In freeing the victim from the force of possession, the family itself is likewise saved from the invasive entity and questions whether it is the power of creation that compels the possessed and frees them from chaos. The endings of these films spotlight the familial paradigm; however, they likewise show the house itself as an emblem that serves as a material memory of the horrors experienced within and the permeability, vulnerability, and transformative ability of bodies, human and domestic.

Stuart Rosenberg's 1979 film *The Amityville Horror* illustrates this concept. Kathy (Margot Kidder) and George Lutz (James Brolin) purchase their first home together. The milestone of homeownership is made even more significant as it is meant to represent a unified, cohesive family; George is the stepfather to Kathy's three children and is anxiously waiting for them to refer to him as a father and not just a man romantically involved with their mother. Though the possession mostly targets George, Kathy's relationship with her children is also highlighted as she navigates her maternal and romantic roles in the shared home. The film complicates the prescribed notions of womanhood by presenting Kathy with an impossible choice. Instead of being wife to George and mother to her children, Kathy must decide to be either wife or mother.

The challenge to parental, domestic roles and responsibilities is again featured in *Insidious* (2010) and *Insidious: Chapter 2* (2013). The two films also focus on issues of motherhood and empowerment in the wake of possession of the male characters. *Insidious* concentrates on Dalton (Ty Simpkin) and his mysterious coma. It turns out that he is not actually comatose; instead, his soul is distanced from his body in another dimension, known as the Further. In order to get Dalton back into his body and for his body to not become possessed by a demon, his father, Josh (Patrick Wilson), must enter the Further to find his son and bring him back to the land of the living. Prior to this otherworldly rescue mission, Josh was largely the inactive parent; instead, Renai (Rose Byrne), the mother, was the one most active in the home and with the children. She was the first one awake in the morning and the one primarily responsible for the family's well-being while Josh distanced himself at work.

Insidious and *Insidious: Chapter 2* go beyond examining the unstable family by destabilizing the concept of the home itself. We tend to think of homes as stable constructs situated in reality. The *Insidious* films purposely make the audience constantly question which home, at what time, in what reality we view them by reimagining homes as tangible and abstract, fixed and fluid. This is characteristic of post-9/11 horror, as Bernice M. Murphy explains:

> This recurrent depiction of the family home as an inherently insecure milieu ripe for invasion by sinister forces also taps into the kind of powerful uncertainty which increasingly characterizes middle-class life in the United States. This feeling of instability is further emphasized by the fact that the demonic entities in each film considered here are ultimately successful in their attempts to break through. . . . The films further emphasize that the assumed stability of the American family unit is always under threat, and that loved ones can be "taken over" by forces that want nothing other than to cause pain and despair. This strain of insecurity within the nuclear family is also one that can be linked to the resonant undercurrent of economic anxiety contained in the films. (240–41)

This instability adds to the horror of the film since, at any moment, the family could be under attack. At first, Renai believes the house to be the problem; however, the family soon learns that it's not the house that's haunted, it's humans.

The house, however, is very much haunted in *The Conjuring* (2013) and *The Conjuring 2* (2016). The films likewise transfer the haunting from the house to a character through the act of possession. Much like *The Amityville Horror*, *The Conjuring* centers on a family who moves into a haunted house. Based on the real-life Harrisville haunting, the Perron family discover that their newly purchased home is filled with ghosts, the most problematic of which is the ghost of a woman who killed herself and possesses mothers to kill their children before taking their own lives. To save Carolyn (Lili Taylor) from continuing this legacy, Lorraine (Vera Farmiga) calls upon Carolyn to use her maternal agency to expel the ghost from her body.

The Conjuring 2 follows a similar format to the original in being based off of a real-life case: the Enfield haunting in England. There are, in fact, two characters who are the most haunted in this film: Janet (Madison Wolfe), the girl who becomes possessed by the spirit Bill Wilkins (Bob Adrian) and the demon Valak (Bonnie Aarons); and Lorraine herself, who is traumatized by a vision of Ed's (Patrick Wilson) death that the demon showed her as a warning to stop interfering in cases. Her fear takes away her psychic abilities, and to be able to help Janet, Lorraine reclaims her agency to exorcise the demon and save both Ed and Janet.

The Conjuring and *The Conjuring 2* draw from the found-footage genre, in which the plot is presented as a series of video recordings that document the supernatural unfolding. Before the Perron family is even introduced in the first film, we see an interview about a different haunting: the Annabelle doll. The footage ends with Ed reassuringly saying that he and Lorraine can help before cutting to show the pair onstage speaking at a college. *The Conjuring 2* starts with Ed and Lorraine speaking on a television program and questioned by a skeptic. Both films include messages before and after the movie providing background on the cases. At the end of each, photographs and recordings from the documented cases play. The effect of including this documentation is to add credibility and, in doing so, horror to the films by situating them as adaptations of reality. Thus, the mother possessed in *The Conjuring* and the daughter possessed in *The Conjuring 2* are meant to heighten the threat of possession and its destructive nature: instead of life imitating art, it is art reenacting life.

POSSESSION AS TRANSFORMATION:
ROSEMARY'S BABY (1968) AND *THE WITCH* (2016)

One of the ways in which possession disrupts is through the transformation process whereby even the thought of pregnancy can possess a woman; the resulting fetus and, later, baby complete the process to contract a woman into the defining role of mother.[2] Through the possession, an individual becomes increasingly changed from their individual self into the shared space of motherhood. We see this play out in Roman Polanski's *Rosemary's Baby* when Rosemary (Mia Farrow) becomes pregnant with the antichrist. Her pregnancy is her possession as she obsesses over her newly envisioned life as a mother at the expense of her health only to realize it was all part of a satanic coven's plan. Rosemary exemplifies the concept of the feminine mystique:

> The feminine mystique says that the highest value and the only commitment for women is the fulfillment of their own femininity. . . . The new image in this mystique gives to American women the old image: "Occupation: house-wife." The new mystique makes the housewife-mothers, who never had a chance to be anything else, the model for all women. . . . They have no vision of the future, except to have a baby. The only active growing figure in their

world is the child. The housewife heroines are forever young, because their own image *ends* in childbirth. (Friedan 91–93)

Even the title of the film alludes to Rosemary's transformation into a paradigm of motherhood as she comes to be defined by her pregnancy and baby. Although she delights at the pregnancy at first, she is made to physically and mentally suffer as she prepares for her role as mother to the child. The film's attention to the excruciating pains she endures make the loneliness of her situation all the more harrowing. She alone must suffer because she alone is the bringer of the child. The resulting chaos of her reality is made even more apparent by the implied appearance of her unholy child that both horrifies and delights. The film ends as Rosemary accepts her child and her identity as its mother, her role fulfilled. At first repulsed by it, Rosemary quickly realizes that the child is hers: her progeny that reaffirms her procreative purpose.

The pressure to be the ideal woman according to society at the time is a prominent theme in Robert Eggers's *The Witch*. Like *Rosemary's Baby*, the transformation that takes place in *The Witch* is the result of many disruptive scenes that build up to the ending. Thomasin (Anya Taylor-Joy) is contrasted with her mother (Kate Dickie) in appearance and faith, a source of strife on the family farm when she is expected to act as a surrogate maternal figurehead. Banished by the community due to the father's (Ralph Ineson) insolence, the family must start over in an open field. In coming together as a newly formed community, the family resumes the persecution they themselves fled from in accusing Thomasin of witchcraft. In the end, however, she proves them correct as she kills her mother and turns to the devil for freedom.[3] The film depicts witchcraft as a means of escape for women like Thomasin. Shunned by her family and only valued for her servitude to them, it is no wonder that she signs her name in exchange for the better life she never had. It presents the patriarchy of Christianity and the family as one whose power hurts women and families. The devil seems more delightful in comparison.

A Mother's Fight: *The Exorcist* (1973), *The Babadook* (2014), and *Hereditary* (2018)

The Exorcist was first released in 1973 at a time when violent images from the Vietnam War played on the television and the hippie movement began to decline. Americans were more disillusioned with the government because of the war and more distrustful of authority in general. It was also a time when the country saw increased divorce rates and single mothers due to no-fault divorce laws in many states. Divorce is one of the main factors that contributes to Regan's (Linda Blair) possession in the film as the return of the father in spiritual form saves the family. Regan's mother, Chris (Ellen Burstyn), is a nontraditional mother: she is single, has an ambitious career as an actress, and openly, passionately swears. The first time we see Chris is at night when she is writing notes in a script before checking on her sleeping daughter, presenting the conflict between her work and personal life from the start. Regan's possession challenges her mother through forced attempts to distance Chris from her daughter. While it is the father, Father Karras (Jason Miller), who ultimately saves Regan, none of it would have been possible had it not been for Chris's fight for her daughter's life. Because of that, the film can be read as transforming motherhood from a controlled state to that of one with disruptive agency, going so far as to push back against the Catholic Church.

For Amelia (Essie Davis), this disruptive agency serves as the catalyst to rebuild her relationship with her son. Amelia's possession in *The Babadook* is less by an external monster and more by her internal trauma from the death of her husband. Oskar (Benjamin Winspear) died while driving her to the hospital to give birth to their son, Samuel (Noah Wiseman). Amelia struggles with both the trauma of losing her husband and the difficulty of being a single mother to an unruly, at times, disobedient, child. The monster who possesses Amelia, the Babadook, exploits this trauma to try to have Amelia kill her son. Samuel helps his mother remember who she is supposed to be, and it is through reclaiming and redefining her maternal role that Amelia is able to expel and contain the monster, thus taking back control over life.

Like the Babadook itself, the monster in *Hereditary*, as the name suggests, is connected to family. Try as protagonist Annie (Toni Collette) does to stop her mother (Kathleen Chalfant) from achieving her goal of fully resurrecting the god Paimon, Annie is unable to. The film follows Annie's suffering as she loses her mother, daughter, and her head as supernatural forces possess and consume the family. In the end, the family becomes no more than one of Annie's figurines in an exhibit, players in the larger spectacle of possession and resurrection.

Chapter Overview

This book looks at the aforementioned ten possession films: *Rosemary's Baby*, *The Exorcist*, *The Amityville Horror*, *Insidious* and *Insidious: Chapter 2*, *The Conjuring* and *The Conjuring 2*, *The Babadook*, *The Witch*, and *Hereditary*. The chapters are in chronological order based on their release date, with the exception of the sequels to *Insidious* and *The Conjuring*; the analyses of the sequels are kept with their predecessors to show the commonalities between each set of films. I chose to organize the chapters chronologically since it better shows the changing depictions of women, motherhood, and children in possession films throughout the years, noting the complexities surrounding modern-day maternity.[4]

The films themselves were chosen because each spotlights a narrower aspect of this larger topic of the intersection of gender, the domestic, and horror. *Rosemary's Baby* concentrates on issues of pregnancy and birth, introducing my discussion of the patriarchal medical institution's treatment of the female body. The film corresponds to history at the time:

> The supernatural horror movie of the 1970s, however, stands apart in its close ties to the historical context of that decade and the years directly preceding it. *The Exorcist* and the films that followed it were consumed within that specific post-Watergate and post-Vietnam context but were, in truth, responding to earlier panic surrounding societal disintegration and endangered youth, originating in the intergenerational turmoil and social change of the late 1960s and frequently intersecting with the supernatural or "the occult." From the sexual exploitation of minors to the counterculture and drug usage, from experimentation with alternative belief systems to cults and motorcycle gangs, the young appeared to many of their elders as being intent upon unleashing both secular and spiritual anarchy. (Beard 214)

My reading of *The Exorcist* continues this discussion by commenting on the film's incorporation of the likewise patriarchal religious institution as a complement to the medical treatment of Regan's body, demonstrating that it is ultimately the return of the paternal that saves Regan in the end. My chapter on *The Exorcist* explains the significance of the physical structure of the Georgetown home as a reflection of the deeper plot points in the film, laying the foundation for the deeper exploration of architecture throughout the proceeding chapters.

I acknowledge the time gap between *The Amityville Horror* and the discussion of my first contemporary horror film, *Insidious*. *The Amityville Horror* was first released in 1979, five years after *The Texas Chainsaw Massacre* (1974) and only one year after *Halloween* (1978). Both of those helped usher in the era of slasher movies that would dominate well into the 1980s, with popular films such as *Friday the 13th* (1980) and *Nightmare on Elm Street* (1984). The demon child featured in horror of the 1960s and '70s in *Rosemary's Baby* (1968), *The Exorcist* (1973), and *The Omen* (1976) became less prominent in 1980s and '90s horror, which tended to focus more on blood and gore in films like *Hellraiser* (1987) and *Candyman* (1992), in addition to featuring adaptations of previously published characters and works in the case of *It* (1990), *The Silence of the Lambs* (1991), and *Interview with the Vampire* (1994). Late 1990s and 2000s horror was largely marked by the rise of the torture-porn genre in films such as Takashi Miike's *Audition* (1999), James Wan's *Saw* (2004), and Eli Roth's *Hostel* (2005), as well as in found-footage movies such as Hideo Nakata's 1998 *Ringu* (*The Ring*, directed by Gore Verbinski, was released in 2002), Eduardo Sánchez and Daniel Myrick's *The Blair Witch Project* (1999), and Oren Peli's *Paranormal Activity* (2007).

I revisit the house as a physical body in my chapters on *The Amityville Horror* and *Insidious/Insidious: Chapter 2* to look into the ways in which the physical structure of the domestic comes to reflect the internal structure of selfhood. *The Conjuring* adds to this by exemplifying the horror trope known as the housing-crisis trope, one that stresses a return to classical aesthetic elements situated within the domestic. *The Conjuring 2* incorporates this connection between material objects and possession as well, initially linking the family armchair to what is perceived to be the demonic spirit possessing the youngest daughter. While the material is certainly an element in *The Conjuring 2*, the film deals more directly with socioeconomic challenges to single motherhood, with single mother Peggy and her children the ones experiencing supernatural events. Women's authority in male-dominated spheres is contested, with Lorraine doubting her supernatural abilities and agency in protecting others. The films resolve these issues through a feminist reclaiming of power and space.

Meanwhile, it is trauma that produces fear in Jennifer Kent's *The Babadook*. Amelia Vanek, the main character in the movie, is forced to confront and accept the trauma of her motherhood in the film. The film closely links her trauma to the monster's presence; just as her trauma cannot be erased, neither can the monster be defeated. Because the film shows the monster as simply contained in the confines of the basement at the end, it exemplifies Cohen's theory that monsters "can be pushed to the farthest margins of geography and discourse, hidden away at the edges of the world and in the forbidden recesses of our mind, but they always return. And when they come back . . . they bear self-knowledge, *human* knowledge—and a discourse all the more sacred as it arises from the Outside" (20, emphasis original). The chapter on *The Babadook* draws on Cathy Caruth's theory of trauma to show the progression of Amelia's understanding of her trauma. While she tries to initially repress and deny it to keep up the façade of composed motherhood, it comes back to literally haunt her.

Lastly, my chapter on *Hereditary* revolves around the relationships between Annie, the main character, and her family—her mother, husband, and children—to show the performativity of motherhood, the differing outward perception of self a mother enacts in the company of others. I look into the film's fascination with the three main houses—the tree house, the main house, and the various miniature houses Annie creates—to show how the events that take place in each destructure contemporary notions of motherhood.

Concluding Thoughts

Motherhood is a constant state of possession. Mothers are possessed by children, spouses, and other entities that seek to control their bodies and beings. Children, too, can be said to be possessed as their perpetually in-flux bodies and morphing identities put them in continual transformation. This book aims to explore what happens when monsters are added to this already tumultuous mix. Each chapter is meant to peel back the skin of these relationships and reveal the inner battle for the structure of the self.

Too often, however, the self is sublimated into that of a shared space where children, fathers, and others can lay claim to the individual in question. Possession, then, acts to sever these ties, these symbolic umbilical cords, to bind the individual to themselves. Bound by possession, the mother is in a state of regressive reflection by being forced into an invisible womb. In order to survive and reclaim their personhood, the individual must either climb out and reclaim their selfhood or be brought back into existence with rupturing force.

Either way, the self that emerges is not the same as before. Society will still view the individual as mother or child. Possession, however, changes those roles through permanently altering the structure of the self. Possession throws bodies into chaos, violating their sense of internal intimacy. The process of possession makes the individual a spectacle and leaves them raw and open, at the mercy of the forces surrounding them.

CHAPTER 1

Possessed by Pregnancy
Rosemary's Baby

A city skyline and a lullaby. These are the images that open Roman Polanski's 1968 film *Rosemary's Baby*. Adapted from the Ira Levin novel (1967) of the same name, the movie invites the audience to view New York City from an outsider perspective before entering its microcosm and the inhabitants at the center of the film. The film is set in 1965 and reflects much of the anxiety surrounding the revolutionary and tumultuous changes in American culture and society. Youth culture pushed back against the traditional norm of stability associated with the nuclear family that charged the husband/father with many of the family's decisions. Traditional values were seen as under attack while the increased status of fetuses as persons strengthened and echoed conservative roots. At the same time, a popular image for cinematic horror was introduced: the demon fetus or child (Hoffman 244). Carrying this child is the mother condemned to have her pregnancy, her body, made into a controlled spectacle while throwing her into unknowing chaos. In the end, who she was before the child no longer remains; rather, it is now her maternal role that enshrines her.

Issues of pregnancy and motherhood are framed around domesticity and career. At first, Guy (John Cassavetes) and Rosemary Woodhouse are a seemingly ordinary married couple looking for an apartment in the city. Guy is an actor best known for minor roles in plays and for being the star of a Yamaha commercial. It is unclear what Rosemary's background is other than her identity as Guy's wife and the envisioned mother of their future children. They tour the Bramford apartment building and immediately fall in love. It is located close to all the theaters for Guy and is large enough for them to start a family, one day, for Rosemary. The realtor emphasizes that one room could be a nursery and the abundance of closets to show the potential for the couple to grow into the space. The couple quickly takes the apartment; however, their finances and the very cost of the apartment are never revealed. What is revealed is the building's dark past: it was once home to the Trench sisters, "two proper Victorian young ladies" who ate children, and to Adrian Marcato, a man who claimed to have summoned the devil. The contrast between the idealized version of the space that the realtor shows and the historical realities foreshadow much of the film's narrative as Rosemary and Guy progress in their maternal and professional ambitions due to the nefarious influences surrounding them.[1]

SEPARATE BUT CONNECTED

The film can be seen as a critique of both the sexual revolution and the political undercurrent of American society. Guy and Rosemary's neighbors, the Castevets, provide a sharp contrast to the young couple. Guy and Rosemary are young, amorous, and fresh; Roman (Sidney Blackmer) and Minnie (Ruth Gordon) are older, quarrelsome, and outdated. Rosemary styles their apartment with bright colors and new furniture she finds in magazines and catalogues, providing a sharp contrast to the dark colors and antiques found in the Castevets' residence. Guy is insecure and expressive; Roman is confident and reserved. Rosemary is sprightly and bright; Minnie is critical and exaggerated. These contrasts are shown in the very naming of the characters. Guy is only ever referred to as Guy, a name symbolic of the everyday, easily forgettable man who would need an act of divine—or, in this case, unholy—intervention to raise him up in society. Rosemary's name itself is a rustic herb, and she describes herself as a "country girl at heart." Minnie's name can be understood as representing the miniature; wife to Roman, she is a smaller version of him.[2] The name Castevet is implicitly akin to the word "caste," a system of rank and privilege, and "cast" as a verb; both meanings come into play as the Castevets use magic to help bring the antichrist into the world and secure positions of power. Woodhouse, in contrast, is a name that can be associated with a wooden structure, one susceptible to flame.

Roman Castevet's name is an anagram of his birth name, Steven Marcato. He changed it to distance himself from the scandal involving his father, Adrian Marcato, who was accused of witchcraft and killed by a mob. In remaking his name, he likewise remade his identity. As Roman, he is his own individual, the leader of the coven and thus the authority. Roman is likewise a purposeful choice as a name, one that easily brings to mind the Roman Empire, a force that dominated the globe for many years. As leader of the coven, he orchestrates the ritual that allows the devil to come to Earth to impregnate a human woman, an unholy version of the Christian account of the Holy Spirit entering Mary to make her the mother of Jesus.

It is later revealed that the Woodhouses' apartment used to be the back part of the Castevets', their satanist next-door neighbors. This fact reveals that the apartment was never truly their own but an extension from the older, larger apartment, symbolic of their generation. Rhona Berenstein comments on this significance:

> Rosemary's and Guy's apartment, instead of forming a self-contained unit, becomes a sort of vaginal passage from the Castevet's place, not merely into Rosemary's body (i.e. as a body carrying a child), but also into her body as a birth canal (creating a continuity between the mother delivering her child and the devil's workers). And though she travels outside her apartment, the residue of the coven's actions follows her there. (66)

Berenstein continues: "The coven members intervene in Guy's and Rosemary's coupling from the beginning of the film—suggesting that the nuclear family is indeed one of the film's primary targets. Minnie's and Roman's voices echo in Guy's and Rosemary's bedroom on their first night in the apartment, setting a precedent for a string of bedroom and dream interventions" (61). That this interference occurs during the first night in the apartment intertwines the themes of consumerism and sex as Minnie subsequently invites herself into their space to inspect and inquire about purchases, including groceries, while feeding Rosemary cakes and drinks from her own apartment. Although this might seem like a goodhearted gesture, Minnie has taken control of the space to feed and care for Rosemary to groom her for her role as sexual sacrifice and vessel for the unborn antichrist.

Rosemary undertakes the task of completely renovating and furnishing the space. Scenes include stripping wallpaper, painting the walls a bright white, and installing new carpet. The labor involved in these tasks is not undertaken by Rosemary; instead, it is hired carpenters and painters who perform these responsibilities while Rosemary supervises. In one scene, Minnie enters the apartment to marvel at a couch, which Rosemary informs her is new. Minnie continues to snoop around the apartment, picking up the mail, inspecting furniture and cans in the kitchen, all while asking about the price of each item. This scene is carefully placed before the one in which Rosemary and Guy go over to the Castevets' apartment for dinner. It is implied that, after this dinner, Roman approaches Guy with the idea of a trade: impregnating Rosemary with the devil's spawn in exchange for career success for Guy.

The audience is not privy to their conversation and is instead shown Rosemary and Minnie's conversation in the kitchen. In fact, the movie plays with what is made known and unknown to the audience; in doing so, the viewer adopts Rosemary's perspective because of the limited information. Rosemary mentions to Minnie that she comes from a "fertile" family and that she is the aunt of sixteen nieces and nephews. The next day, Minnie invites herself into the Woodhouses' apartment to sit, knit, and chat. She gifts Rosemary a tannis-root necklace, the same one she gave to Terry (Victoria Vetri), the first woman they chose to carry Satan's spawn.[3] The organization of these scenes hints at the price Guy pays for his career: selling his wife's body, sexuality, and fertility. As the camera pans to the parlor where Guy and Roman sit, the viewer is drawn to the cloud of smoke that hides the men. The smoky image would again be repeated during Rosemary's rape, linking the two scenes and showing the connection between Rosemary's reproductive agency and the men who regulate it. Once again, limited perspective is used to emphasize that Rosemary has no say over her own body and individuality.

That night, Guy's demeanor changes toward Rosemary by becoming more controlling. He tells her, "If you took it, you ought to wear it" in reference to the tannis-root necklace. In doing so, he is already controlling Rosemary's physical appearance. In the next scene, Guy receives a phone call to let him know that the actor who landed a lead role instead of Guy has suddenly gone blind and Guy now has the lead. Suddenly, Guy's career takes off, leaving Rosemary feeling neglected in the relationship.[4] Guy uses this distance as emotional leverage, placing dozens of vases of red roses throughout the apartment as an apology to Rosemary. Rosemary, giddy at his seemingly newfound commitment to their marriage, happily accepts Guy's floral gift. He says: "I've been tearing my hair out over my career. Let's have a baby. Let's have three babies.

One at a time." This dialogue reveals what is equated to value in the relationship: for Guy, it is his career, for Rosemary, it's a baby. It also depicts Guy as commanding Rosemary's procreation through deciding when they can start to try to conceive; this control is masked as romantic. The abrupt change in topic, from his career to the prospects of procreation, links the two together: Guy's career and the new baby. Rosemary's fertility is used as capital for the couple to gain what each desires. The roses thus transform the apartment into a fertile space in which red blooms represent menstruation. Guy is the one who orchestrates this through his role as controller and consumer. Through purchasing the roses as gifts, Guy purchases Rosemary's body and sexuality.

Guy's control over her body continues as he tracks her period to ensure that she missed it. He bets her a quarter that she is, in fact, pregnant. When she finds out the results of a blood test confirming that she is, she lets Guy know the news by presenting him with a silver quarter when he arrives home that day:

> ROSEMARY: Let's make this a new beginning, a new openness in talking to one another. We haven't been open.
> GUY: It's true. I've been so goddamn self-centered. That's the trouble. You know I love you, don't you, Ro? I swear to God, I'm going to be as open—
> ROSEMARY: It's my fault as much as yours.

The scene has religious undertones, with the silver quarter symbolic of the silver the Romans paid Judas to betray Jesus.[5] In the scene, Guy can be seen as enacting the part of Judas, selling Rosemary to Roman and the Satanists. Rosemary, the self-sacrificing wife, takes part of the blame for the distance in the relationship rather than pointing the finger at Guy. Rosemary's self-guilt, that she hasn't been as open as Guy has, is meant as a mirror of his own guilt; since she is a mirror of Guy, his guilt is therefore her own.

This trade is made even more apparent the night of Rosemary's rape. Right before collapsing from the effects of the drugged chocolate mousse, Guy watches the pope at Yankee Stadium on television, proclaiming that it would be a "great spot for [his] Yamaha commercial." Enraptured with his own narcissism, Guy is more concerned with promoting his image than with the reality of his wife's well-being. His excuses begin to mirror this self-love as he tells Rosemary the reason why she wakes up visibly wounded. He blames the scratches on ragged nails, remarking that the sex "was kind of fun in a necrophile sort of way." This is the second reference to Rosemary's body as lifeless in conjunction with her rape. In taking away her involvement, Rosemary's agency over her sexual desire is stolen from her.

SEX, CONSUMERISM, AND SELF

Sex is highlighted in several scenes and comes to be associated with both Rosemary's fertility and the couple's consumerism. The first night in their apartment, Rosemary candidly tells Guy, "Hey, let's make love." The pair then engage in a ritualistic portrayal of sex: Guy turns off the light and takes his shirt off, Rosemary takes her dress off, Guy takes his socks and jeans off, Rosemary takes her shoes off, and the two finally kiss. At this point in the film, Rosemary does express sexual agency in initiating physical intimacy between them, and in doing so:

> Rosemary functions as both the sexual initiator in their relationship and as the primary source of speculation and information regarding their plans to have a family.... Her role as initiator is reinforced by camera movement and physical touch, as a hand-held camera in close-up follows her as she moves towards Guy. Later, when Guy lies in bed mimicking the agent who showed them the apartment, Rosemary again initiates their contact by rushing into his arms from her chair across the room. (Berenstein 61)

This agency is later repressed as, it becomes clear, the coven sublimates this power to exploit her sexual and maternal desire. The morning after the rape, she wakes with scratches on her arms and back. She clutches the bedsheet to her chest, hiding her breasts and covering her body as she touches the scratches with her wedding-ring-clad hand. In this moment, she realizes that her body and intimate trust were violated by her husband. As her body is objectified for its sexual and reproductive purposes, Rosemary's autonomy and consent are taken away from her so that she becomes a vessel for the baby.

Rosemary's individuality fades as her entire self—physical and internal—is taken over by the fetus. Such a choice is in keeping with attitudes regarding fetal personhood during the time period as "it was also at this point in time that the fetus began to separate from the pregnant woman carrying it; in 1970, the state of California first added the word 'fetus' to its

Penal Code's description of potential murder victims. This paved the way for fetuses to acquire a perhaps disproportionate level of growing level of agency" (Hoffman 241). In addition, "increasingly sophisticated technology granted doctors, lawyers, judges, and people in general—although not pregnant women, whose access to their fetuses is presumably already as intimate as possible—greater access to fetuses and a stronger sense of their potential personhood, with sometimes oppressive effects for pregnant women" (Hoffman 243). The audience never sees an image of the fetus or child after it is born; rather, we are assured of its presence by her physical symptoms.

The audience is assured of the child's supernatural origins by the dreamlike rape sequence, including the naked bystanders and monstrous arm draped around Rosemary's body. During the ritual, Guy wonders if Rosemary can see. Minnie reassures him: "She can't see. As long as she ate the mousse, she can't see nor hear. Like dead." Guy's primary concern is not that his wife is actually awake but if she can see or rather, more specifically, see him and thus reveal his participation. Minnie compares Rosemary's state as akin to the dead; in doing so, the film problematizes the relationship between the fertile female body and pregnancy, suggesting that Rosemary's body is never truly alive and thus has value until she becomes pregnant with the devil child.[6]

Rosemary's visions during the ritual are insights into her subconscious. At the start of the dream, Rosemary is in her underwear on a boat. This quickly turns into a swimsuit, putting her mind much more at ease and alleviating the shame she feels toward her naked body. She sees Hutch (Maurice Evans) and asks if he is also coming on the voyage. He replies: "Catholics only. I wish we weren't bound by these prejudices." This point is significant, harkening back to Rosemary's earlier admission that she is unsure of her religious faith. Her dream sequence involving Hutch, her friend, being excluded due to religious differences deepens her doubt surrounding her faith.[7]

The overlap of Catholicism with the satanic ritual connects with the aftermath from the Second Vatican Council in 1962. One priest reflects: "The Second Vatican Council and the '60s culture shaped our consciences in new ways and broadened our sense of immorality to include racism, injustice to laborers, unjust or undeclared war, classism, and sexism. By the late '60s, communal penance services opened our awareness of the sin committed and tolerated by the community, and helped us to know that little, if any, of our sin was unique" (Stenzel 24). The aftermath of the Second Vatican Council resulted in decisions meant to modernize Catholicism. The mass switched from Latin to English, making it more accessible for parishioners but overhauling centuries of tradition. While many welcomed the renewal and reform, some viewed the decisions as heretical.

The next image shows her naked on a plank of wood being lifted toward a chapel ceiling; however, she does not ascend into religious heaven. Instead, she descends below the deck of the boat, where she is naked on a mattress in the middle of a room with yellow flowers in it. There is a fire crackling in the background, and her elderly neighbors are naked and chanting. Roman uses a long, phallic instrument to write symbols on her body in red as a woman in a long, flowing outfit apologizes for her not feeling well. She recommends tying her legs in case of convulsions, and Rosemary readily agrees. This measure coincides with restraints during sex play in addition to possession imagery; these two readings posit Rosemary's sexual body as possessed by the coven. The devil appears in the shape of Guy, but the difference is made evident due to the demonic hands that graze her legs and body. These hands and arms are scaly and burnt, suggesting a reptilian, monstrous appearance. She opens her eyes to see yellow pupils looking back at her. She screams, "This is no dream; this is really happening!" She climaxes and opens her eyes as someone puts a pillow over her to put her back to sleep. Her sexual agency muted, she is rendered no more than a submissive object for others to inflict their will upon.

The scene and the overall dream sequence represent Rosemary's final departure from her lapsed Catholicism as she opens her body up to the devil and, subsequently, possession. As Berenstein reveals:

> Her nightmare pivots around her nakedness, the nakedness of those around her, her sexual/religious guilt, her impregnation and the construction of that impregnation as spectacle (both for the viewer and for the coven members). The fact that Rosemary's second "dream" becomes a spectacle of intercourse underlines the importance of the act of impregnation i.e. while the scene can be analyzed as the expression of an animal/evil sexuality, it is also Rosemary's pregnancy which is triggered and anxiously implied. Her third dream, quite tame in light of the church's and the devil's absences, centers on the image of Rosemary and her future children, "a happy family in a happy world." (58)

The nightmare purposely blurs with reality to show the contrast between Rosemary's inner self and the external forces that influence and control her.

The dream continues as she sees the pope with a red suitcase. The following conversation takes place between her and the pope:

POPE: They tell me you have been bitten by a mouse.
ROSEMARY: Yes, that's why I couldn't come to see you.
POPE: Oh, that's alright. I wouldn't want you to jeopardize your health.
ROSEMARY: Am I forgiven, Father?
POPE: Oh, absolutely.

The suggested action taking place is Rosemary seeking forgiveness for both her lapsed Catholicism and the carnal element associated with reproduction. When the pope says that she is, in fact, forgiven, he presents her with a ring that is actually the tannis-root charm Minnie gave her. In kissing the tannis-root ring, Rosemary unknowingly pledges herself to the Satanists in order to conceive. The scene also has parallels to the earlier dinner in which she playfully refers to Guy as a father figure by calling him "Daddy" in reference to seeking his approval for eating dessert. The structuring of both scenes illustrates the patriarchal reverence she is trapped within, seeking forgiveness for not being fully submissive toward men's plans.

PATRIARCHAL POSSESSION

From the moment she expresses interest in starting a family, her body is controlled by those around her. Guy insists upon telling Minnie and Roman about the pregnancy; in turn, they insist on Rosemary seeing their friend Abraham Saperstein (Ralph Bellamy) as her doctor. Saperstein, they tell her, "delivers all the society babies" and is "one of the finest obstetricians in the country," appealing to Rosemary's sense of consumerism and status. Minnie calls Saperstein herself to arrange everything, telling him that he is not to charge her "none of your fancy society prices," conveying that the baby alone elevates Rosemary's status. During her first meeting with Saperstein, the doctor tells Rosemary not to read books and not to listen to her friends, citing how each pregnancy is different. He also rejects vitamin pills, saying that he'll have Minnie make her a drink from her herbarium that is "fresher, safer, and more vitamin-rich than any pill on the market." He adds: "Any questions you have, call me night or day, not your Aunt Fanny. That's what I'm here for." His instructions are more commands, ones designed to isolate Rosemary from a community of external support in the form of books and female friends in order to control her mind as well as her body to subjugate her to his care. Yet Rosemary smiles and appreciates his paternal tone.

As her pregnancy continues, she experiences extreme pain. When she asks Saperstein about it, he dismisses it as "probably an expansion of the pelvis. You can fight it with ordinary pain medicine." She expresses her concerns that it could be an ectopic pregnancy, a very real medical condition that no ordinary pain medicine can treat. Rather than take her concerns and pain seriously, Saperstein turns his attention to the fact that she read a book on pregnancy that gave her that suggestion and instructs her to throw the book away since all it did was worry her. She later admits to Guy, "Pain like this is a warning something's wrong." Robin A. Hoffman comments on this: "The image of her bulging abdomen, pregnant with both potential evil and potential child, emphasizes her subordination to her unseen fetus and its external agents. Everyone who sees her comments on her wasted appearance, which suggests that the fetus is really a parasite that is consuming her" (249). Indeed, much of the horror of the film revolves around that which cannot be seen: the growing baby inside of Rosemary, the cause of her pain. This is keeping with available reproductive technology of the time:

> The technology for imaging fetuses *in utero* was far too rare and/or expensive to be a diagnostic tool. Cruelly, Rosemary cannot exploit any imaging technology that would reveal her fetus's true nature, though the prospect of visual confirmation hovers tantalizingly over Rosemary's belly: her own body either protecting the Antichrist or casting suspicion on an innocent and much-desired human fetus. The viewer is left with the sense that Rosemary is paralyzed by her condition and her ignorance about it. . . . Rosemary is chronically reliant upon others for information about her own body, which reinforces her subordination to the contents of her womb: she needs Guy to inform her that her period is late; she needs doctors to confirm her pregnancy and assess her condition; and she needs friends to tell her that her constant pain is a health hazard. (Hoffman 248)

Rosemary's selfhood is gone; instead, she is replaced by her pregnant body. Her own health issues are not concerning as the sign of a growing abdomen shows that the fetus is growing and therefore healthy. She loses weight and becomes pale and skeletal in appearance, with dark shadows under her eyes and her spinal column visible when she bends over. She is possessed by her pregnancy. Her priority and the priority of those around her is the health of the baby, not Rosemary. Rosemary's appearance and the cause of her ailment is meant to disturb and upset the audience by challenging prescribed attitudes of pregnancy that choose to glorify it without addressing the grueling, painful reality that can occur.

Guy contributes to this dismissal of her pain. She tells him that she feels "awful," and he reassures her that she looks "great" while also insulting her new haircut. He emphasizes her physical beauty. In doing so, he redirects her attention toward beauty standards: her haircut takes away from her physical beauty and is therefore the cause of pain. Her hair is cut close to her head, and with her thin frame, her outward appearance is androgenized. Berenstein notes this significance:

> Rosemary is androgynized [*sic*] once her pregnancy is established. After her appointment at Vidal Sassoon . . . her "fashionable" haircut minimizes the signs of her gender. While her growing stomach and maternity dresses signify sexual difference, her haircut, boyish features and the eradication of her sexual desire and desirability . . . point to the neutralization of difference and its replacement by a desexualized androgyny. Rosemary thus acts as an ambiguous figure of motherhood, at once androgynous and simultaneously portraying the archetypal mother who suffers for her child. By minimizing the traditional surface cues of gender difference (costume, ornamentation, make-up and coiffure) [the film exaggerates] the patriarchal schism between culture and nature, between the cultural manifestations of gender and the "natural" mandates of reproduction. (63)

From there, the pregnancy possesses her by altering her physical appearance and subjecting her to the control of the unholy fetus through debilitating pain. By extension, the patriarchal institutions of marriage and medicine at the time also control her, leaving her helpless and alone in her plight. It is the fetus, not Rosemary, that has the power.

Guy's controlling behavior is progressively built up throughout the film. On the night they begin trying for a child, Minnie drops off chocolate mousse, which she terms "chocolate mouse." Rosemary notices a chalky aftertaste to the dish, but Guy dismisses her, saying, "There's no undertaste. Come on, the old bat salved all day. Now, eat it." His rhetoric continues to be peppered with directives toward Rosemary, telling her, "Don't eat it. There's always something wrong" and "Look, if you really can't stand it, just don't eat it." To appease her husband, Rosemary pretends to eat it, tricking him into believing that she finished the dish. When he returns from turning over the record, she asks, "There, Daddy, do I get a gold star?" The line can be read as coyly seductive, given Rosemary's costuming in a bright-red jumpsuit and the occasion for the evening. It can also be seen as infantilizing Rosemary, calling Guy "Daddy" and asking if she gets a reward for doing what he demanded of her.

It is during a party in which she is surrounded by women in the kitchen that she cries to them about the pain and pregnancy. The women purposely block Guy from entering, forming a sisterhood around their friend. They are shocked to find out she has been in pain for months and the doctor has done nothing to stop it. When they suggest that she should see another doctor, she responds: "No, he's very good. He was on *Open-Ed*." Her response shows the link between commercialism and pregnancy, citing a television program as credentials. When one comments that "She can't go on suffering like this," Rosemary cries, "I won't have an abortion!" Her answer shows the problematization of women's pain in the medical field. Her response highlights her understanding of pregnancy as being painful; the removal of pain entails the removal of the fetus.[8] This depiction of pregnancy is terrifying. It draws on social and biblical tenets that women are supposed to suffer for motherhood and that women are marked as damned from the start.

After the guests leave, Rosemary sits in a chair in the living room while Guy stands and paces around her, casting the patriarchal tone of the scene. Rosemary's body language is childlike and guilty, with slouched shoulders and downcast eyes, her hands crossed in front of her stomach. She sits while Guy stands with his hands on his hips. He calls her friends "a bunch of not very bright bitches who ought to mind their own goddamn business!" as his verbal and body language are domineering and threatening. He leans into Rosemary and slams his hands against each other, feigning a punch, as he invades her space and berates her for questioning Dr. Saperstein's medical care. Guy's abuse continues through, at first, appealing to the couple's financial situation in saying that "we'll have to pay Saperstein" if they do not continue to see him. He finally concludes that the idea of Rosemary no longer being a patient of Dr. Saperstein's is "out of the question" and waves his finger at her. He states, "I won't let you do it, Ro . . . it's not fair to Saperstein." Rosemary is

Guy (John Cassavetes) dismisses Rosemary's (Mia Farrow) concerns and takes control.
© Paramount Pictures.

appalled and astonished, crying out, "What about what's fair to me?" This line
is one of the few times in the film Rosemary clearly expresses her repressed
outrage. Even in doing so, however, she clutches her hand to her stomach
in a move that can be seen as defensive by reminding Guy of her value in
being a pregnant body. Guy is shown as Rosemary's abuser and keeper, using
his power to quell his wife's proclaimed independence. He, however, is not
what causes her to reclaim her space as the submissive wife: it is the baby,
kicking inside of her, that reaffirms Rosemary's place in the domestic sphere
and submission to those around her. Feeling the baby kicking and the pain
stopping, Rosemary repeatedly cries, "It's alive!"

After this reassurance, she happily receives her nutritional drink and
cake from Minnie. The film shows a series of more apartment renovations
as she transforms the extra room into a nursery and stocks it with bibs and
a bassinet and outfits the walls with wallpaper. She packs her suitcase for
the hospital. Her happiness is short-lived, however. After receiving a book
about witches, she investigates and finds out that Roman is actually the son of
Adrian Marcato, a famous Satanist who was said to have conjured the devil.
Rosemary becomes suspicious of those she used to trust and seeks refuge
in Dr. Hill (Charles Grodin); her hope is that science and the medical field
can provide sanctuary for the expecting mother. She is betrayed, however, as
she finds that, rather than listening and helping her, Dr. Hill only contacted
Dr. Saperstein and her husband:

DR. SAPERSTEIN: Come with us quietly, Rosemary . . . because if you say any
    more about witches or witchcraft, I'll be forced to take you to a mental
    hospital. You don't want that, do you? So put your shoes on.
GUY: We just want to take you home. No one's going to hurt you.
DR. SAPERSTEIN: Put your shoes on. . . . She's fine now. We're going to go
    home and rest.
DR. HILL: That's all it takes.
DR. SAPERSTEIN: Thank you for your trouble, doctor.
DR. HILL: Glad I could be of help, sir.
GUY: Shame you had to come in here.

The dialogue serves to demonstrate the intertwining of marriage, medicine, and power. Rosemary is rendered helpless and voiceless in this scene. At nine months pregnant and due to give birth the following week, she is physically vulnerable, with her movements reduced by her body. Saperstein and Dr. Hill take away her voice and agency as she is directed how to react and think by the men. Not only does this show the male-dominated medical field's clout but also how women's concerns are dismissed. Rosemary is coerced to go with her captors or else be imprisoned in a mental hospital, a threat that was very real at the time. She can either be crazy or be submissive.

Still, Rosemary does try to escape from those around her. She rushes to the apartment and feels secure behind her locked door. Her apartment is invaded by her elderly neighbors, the members of the coven, and they sneak behind her to hold her down. It is in this apartment that she is forced to give birth because she goes into labor. She is strapped down by the coven, her swollen belly gripped by Saperstein as he counts the seconds between contractions. Her body, space, and intimacy have been completely violated. She is physically overwhelmed by their forces and screams: "Oh, Andy or Jenny, I'm sorry my little darling. Forgive me." She blames herself for what is happening and, in doing so, undermines her earlier expressions of agency.

The audience never sees Rosemary actually give birth to her baby. However, Rosemary is shown drugged, raped, and impregnated by the devil. Lucy Fischer comments on this importance:

On one level (divested of the occult), the scene can be read as a dramatization of old-fashioned home birth—with a female midwife present. The feigned death of Rosemary's child stands in for the infant mortality that obtained until the modern era.... On another tier, the birth scene superimposes upon that historical site the malevolent mythology of witchcraft—the notion of midwives as Satanic, as swiping babies for the devil. On a final plateau, the vignette subjectively replicates woman's experience of traditional hospital birth—of being physically restrained, anesthetized, and summarily separated from her baby. (450–51)

The film is careful not to show the actual birth scene. To do so would be to enter into a space that is not traditionally reserved for men: the birthing room. The choice to omit this scene also speaks to the treatment of women's bodies at the hands of men. Pregnant and nonpregnant bodies are seen, but birthing bodies are taboo. The act of giving birth is regarded as a female spectacle; the female body assumes power as it brings life into the world. The act of labor is just that: work. Work that causes the woman's body to become volatile and dangerous. For the film to deny Rosemary this moment of paramount motherhood and maternal agency places emphasis on the male perspective. We only know Rosemary has given birth by the absence of the physical signs of her pregnancy. The swollen belly is no longer there, and she is instead presented in a cleaned up, composed manner.

When she awakens, it is through her eyes that we see Guy and Dr. Saperstein staring back and down at her in bed. Such a choice invites the audience to feel as Rosemary does: helpless and confined. Later, the film adopts her gaze when she invades the Castevets' apartment to search for her missing baby. Hoffman comments on this cinematic choice: "The camera adopts Rosemary's viewpoint at crucial moments in the film: As a result, her concern for her baby becomes the audience's concern, and we also struggle, reluctantly, to accept the reality of both Satanists and conspiracy within the film" (247). Inside of the Castevets' apartment, the audience is again invited to view the unfolding horror as Rosemary does. She is kept in her bedroom, in bed. She is not allowed to walk around and is visited first by her husband and then by Saperstein. Saperstein delivers the news of the birth:

ROSEMARY: Where is it? The baby, where is it? Where's my baby? Where's the baby? Where is it?
DR. SAPERSTEIN: There were complications, Rosemary, but nothing that will affect future births.
ROSEMARY: It's . . .

DR. SAPERSTEIN [wiping glasses]: Dead . . . At a hospital, I might have been able
    to do something about it, but you can start out again in a very few months.
GUY: As soon as you're better.
ROSEMARY: I don't believe you. You're both lying! You're lying! It didn't die! You
    took it! You're lying! You witches! You're lying! You're lying! You're lying!

Even with the news that her child is supposed to be dead, Saperstein directs
blame to Rosemary. He implies that her escape attempt prompted the home
delivery as opposed to the planned hospital one. She is denied postpartum support from her doctor, who only prescribes pills to keep her calm and sedated
while neighbors bring her food and have her pump her breastmilk for them
to take away. Not only is this meant to keep her quiet and controlled, it is also
meant to control the leaking body through regulating the lactation process.

Guy's dialogue emphasizes this lack of support when he degrades her
condition, saying she was "really ka-pow out of [her] mind" and that she had
the "prepartum crazies." He assures her that all she needs to do is "rest and
get over them." He continues:

I know this is the worst thing that's ever happened to you, but from now on,
everything's going to be roses. Paramount is within an inch of where we want
them and suddenly Universal is interested, too. We're going to blow this town
and be in the beautiful hills of Beverly with a pool and a spice garden, the
whole schmear. And two kids . . . Gotta run, get famous.

He eats the food from her tray while speaking to her to underplay the seri-
ousness of his wife's health and invades her space. She simply needs to rest
and awaken to a new reality for the pair of them in which Guy is famous
and they can live his dream life, which he compares to food that they can
consume by calling it "schmear." His reference to roses is significant as they
are displayed throughout the film. He decorates the apartment in red roses as
an apology and to propose that they start a family. During her rape, Rosemary
lays on a mattress with roses printed on it. His line serves to bring attention to
Rosemary's fertility and his own ambition. He later tells her: "They promised
me you wouldn't be hurt, and you haven't been. Really. I mean, suppose you
had the baby and you lost it. Wouldn't that be the same? Gained so much
in return." He achieved the fame he always craved, while she is left with the
trauma from the pregnancy and birth.

Betrayed by those around her, Rosemary finally takes control of her situation. She grabs a butcher knife from the kitchen, and wielding the phallic symbol of power, she enters Minnie and Roman's apartment through the connecting linen closet. In the parlor, she sees the party taking place celebrating the birth of the satanic baby, her baby, resting in a black basinet with an upside-down crucifix. As Roman shouts, "Hail, Satan!" and tells her the truth behind the child's father, Rosemary is terrified, shocked, and overcome by emotion. As T. S. Kord writes: "She receives no sympathy or support from anyone; in fact, her husband, neighbors and doctor conspire to force her into unwilling motherhood. Scenes showing a desperate Rosemary approaching the cradle with a large carving knife stunningly symbolize the guilt that may be felt by involuntary mothers" (114). Minnie reaches out to her, reminding her of the so-called honor she holds: "He chose you out of all the world; out of all the women in the whole world, he chose you! He wanted you to be the mother of his only living son!" Her words remind Rosemary of constructed maternal privilege: that a man, or masculine entity, choosing her to be the mother of his child should be considered the highest achievement for a woman. In reality, however, Rosemary is not special; she is just the available body. Terry was the first choice before she took her own life. It is in this final reveal that the film highlights Rosemary's detachment from her own body and agency at the hands of those around her. In doing so, we see that Rosemary's role was never her own; rather, she was always a puppet controlled by men meant to play whatever role they gave her.

The scene also subverts what should be seen as taboo: the unholy reunion of mother and demon child. Instead, the scene codifies the satanic triumph that "God is dead! Satan lives!" as normal and celebratory, while casting the monstrous element with Rosemary through her initial rejection of her baby. She asks, "Are you trying to get me to be his mother?" Her question shows her separation from the child. Roman encourages her to be a mother to her baby not out of maternal love but to help out the coven with the endeavor. Clad in an oversized, light-blue housecoat, Rosemary stands out against the stark-black cloth of the bassinet. The contrast demonstrates Rosemary's transformation into the baby's mother. Indeed, the audience and the coven have Rosemary's answer as she rocks the bassinet and tends to her baby, with the final music of the film being the lullaby melody heard at the beginning.

The ending can be seen as an attack on Catholicism as the Satanists celebrate their triumph. A *Time* magazine cover in Dr. Saperstein's office asks, "Is

Roman (Sidney Blackmer) offers Rosemary a chance at motherhood. © Paramount Pictures.

God Dead?" Roman critiques Catholicism in a comparison to show business with its ritual and costumes. He tells Rosemary that she does not have to respect the pope as he only pretends to be holy. Minnie remarks about the cost of the jewels and roses. While these are all critiques, the Satanists also display similar characteristics. The rape and impregnation of Rosemary is highly ritualistic and stylized. Minnie and Roman's apartment, the meeting place of the Satanists, has dark wood and shining silver. Minnie's fetish with the cost of items shows her hunger for those goods. Indeed, Roman's name can be read as a play on the Roman Empire, with him acting as a leader expanding his power.

The film's ending leaves the viewer wondering about Rosemary's future. In spitting in her husband's eye, she seemingly rejects him and his vision of the future for the pair of them to stay with her child. Yet it is also made clear that not all the coven welcomes her involvement despite Roman's invitation. Her nonsensical lullaby, "la-la-la" both harkens to her role as the baby's mother and the destabilization of her mental state and her acceptance of motherhood. The film thus leaves the viewer in the same place they started: Rosemary invisible onscreen, her voice drifting into the background. We do not need to know what happens after this. Rosemary has served her purpose. After all, the film is not called "Rosemary." It's called *Rosemary's Baby*.

From this film comes other cinematic progeny that further evolve the issues surrounding gender, pregnancy, and motherhood. Stewart Thorndike's 2014 film *Lyle* pushes *Rosemary's Baby* in new directions through its exploration of grief, postpartum depression, and pregnancy. Like Rosemary, Leah (Gaby Hoffmann) is faced with a pregnancy that she suspects is being controlled by nefarious forces. Leah's pregnancy is also marked by loss of her first born, Lyle, whose death is a sacrifice to change the sex of the fetus from a girl to a boy. This fulfills the desire of her partner, June (Ingrid Jungermann), for a boy, which ensures June's success via a devilish pact. John Lee's *False Positive* (2021) likewise pushes the boundaries of motherhood through Lucy's (Ilana Glazer) pregnancy, which is completely controlled by her doctor (Pierce Brosnan) from its inception. *False Positive* removes the supernatural element and instead focuses on how the medical field can entrap women by her doctor inseminating her with his sperm, not her husband's, and terminating, without consent, the female fetus so that the two male fetuses can survive.

Rosemary's Baby and its adaptations all highlight how a woman's desire to be a mother can be used against her. Rather than claiming the pregnancy and child as their own, mothers can instead be subjugated by men taking control of their babies, bodies, and selves. Unlike Rosemary, these women do not become submissive. Their screams are battle cries that they will not be silenced.

CHAPTER 2

Puberty as Hell
The Exorcist

While it is the mother possessed in *Rosemary's Baby*, *The Exorcist* approaches possession differently through the daughter being possessed and the mother being forced to bear witness as the demon lays ruin to her otherwise composed daughter's body and self. This decomposition, in turn, destabilizes the mother's control over her daughter. The film centers around Regan MacNeil, a twelve-year-old girl who becomes possessed by the demon Pazuzu after playing with a Ouija board in the Georgetown home she and her mother, Chris, stay in while Chris stars in a movie filming in the city. Regan's possession can be seen as a backlash to the climate in which she lives in. The beginning of the film suggests that the demon was always in the house, with the attic and basement playing an important role in implying the demon's presence. The audience's first glimpse into the home is Chris waking up to hear scratching from the attic before checking on her sleeping daughter in the bedroom across the hall, just steps away from the attic door. The sounds from the attic increase, and when Chris investigates, she finds no evidence of rats as she previously supposed; it is unclear what the origin of the noises are, but a supernatural presence is made visible when the flicker of Chris's candle suddenly bursts into a wave of flames. Later, when Chris visits Regan in the basement to see her daughter's latest craft, she finds the Ouija board her daughter played with to contact a spirit simply known as Captain Howdy, a spirit that speaks telepathically to Regan. Regan's mother is shown as unable to protect her daughter from the horrors that ensue in the home; rather, it is the return of the father figure and paternal power that saves Regan in the end.

Chris stars in a film as a professor who joins student protests over a building being torn down on a fictional campus. The oppression of the higher administration, the angry and disgruntled students, and Chris's character's own criticism at the institution correlate to real-world events taking place at the time. Drew Beard writes:

> At the same time, an increasingly pervasive atmosphere of pessimism and cynicism followed highly publicized corruption in government and loss of faith in elected officials and leaders (most notably, the Watergate scandal and the resignation of President Richard Nixon). Meanwhile, the Vietnam War continued and was accompanied back in the United States by inflation, recession, unemployment, and energy shortages resulting from the 1973 OPEC oil embargo, leading to gas lines and shortages at the pump, creating a sense of a soft or weakened nation, vulnerable to manipulation and attack from hostile outside forces, uncannily similar to the protagonists of *The Exorcist* and other 1970s-era supernatural horror movies. (214–15)

These concerns are reflected in the film through Regan's possession and subsequent exorcism. At first, she appears as a young girl beginning puberty. Her possession is a gradual transformation of her body, fueled by the disruptive transition between childhood and adolescence and her tumultuous homelife: her parents are divorced, and her mother employs staff to care for Regan in her absence.

The location and design of the house become important in the film as both the nature of the internal and external aspects of the house correspond to the events leading up to and during the exorcism. Because of its location in a city versus a more rural setting, "the relationship between house and space becomes an artificial one. Everything about it is mechanical and, on every side, intimate living flees" (Bachelard 27). Inside the house, the attic and basement become sites of the initial supernatural events and establish a verticality to the home. Gaston Bachelard outlines two key concepts regarding homes and intimacy in his work *The Poetics of Space: The Classic Look at How We Experience Intimate Places*: "1. A house is imagined as a vertical being. It rises upward. . . . 2. A house is imagined as a concentrated being. It appeals to our consciousness of centrality" (17). He elaborates on this concept of verticality, saying, "Verticality is ensured by the polarity of cellar and attic" and that "in the attic, fears are easily 'rationalized.' Whereas in the cellar . . . 'rationalization' is less rapid and less clear; also, it is never *definitive*. In the attic, the day's experiences can always efface the fears of night. In the cellar, darkness prevails both day and night, and even when we are carrying a lighted candle, we see shadows dancing on the dark walls" (Bachelard 17, 19, emphasis original). Symbolically, the attic is associated with the act of ascending a space; for a malevolent presence to then inhabit it subverts the sanctity of it and thus the house itself. Likewise, the cellar is a space in which a person descends; it is there that Chris discovers the Ouija board her daughter has been playing with, communicating with an unfamiliar, and thus dangerous, spirit.[1]

If the attic and cellar are the opposite points of verticality, then the central sites are the parlor downstairs and Regan's bedroom upstairs, closest to the attic. These sites then become prime locations of acts of Regan's possession and help to illustrate Regan as the popular child-as-monster trope in horror films that Andrew Scahill refers to as the "revolting child." He states:

> The child is exponentially troubling, as s/he seems to have no need for the entry into "adulthood," which is to say, normative development. The coming-of-age tale becomes horribly refigured as the already-of-age tale, as monstrous children claim violent rage, libidinal agency, and inappropriate knowledge assumed to be the solitary domain of adulthood. As such, the revolting child represents the failure of "proper" development, in which children successfully sublimate infantile desires and drives into the proper outlets to enter a nascent adulthood. (Scahill 41)

The position of Regan's bedroom in the house likewise illustrates her status as the revolting child. Her bedroom is located at the top of the home, away from her mother's bedroom and farthest away from the body of the house, the downstairs where Chris entertains and greets visitors. In one of the film's most iconic scenes, Regan spider walks down the stairs backwards, perverting the ordinary, domestic space with the spectacle of her abnormality.[2] In another scene, she interrupts her mother's party by standing in the doorway of the parlor and urinating, physically and symbolically claiming the space; clad in a nightgown, it is clear that her mother meant for her to be sequestered in her bedroom, up above and far away from the lively adults below.

By placing her bedroom in this location, Regan emblematizes the mad-woman in the attic even before her possession; she is already Othered by the burgeoning adolescence her mother struggles to accept. Regan uses her position at the top of the home to her advantage in her possessed state, throwing her mother's romantic interest from the window onto the steps below, thus expelling and rejecting the invasive male presence. The method of his murder, being thrown from the window atop the home, highlights the ejection of the male from Regan's psyche and her retention of control over the power of the house.

MOTHER, DAUGHTER DEMONIZED

The film establishes Regan and Chris's relationship as one in which the single mother is stigmatized for failing to protect the child. Chris MacNeil is por-trayed as an abject mother by going against traditional models of mother-hood. She is divorced, single, and openly swears. She disagrees with her male director about her role in a film, playing a professor who protests a building that's set to be torn down. In her professional and personal lives, she revolts and rebels. Chris awakens from a phone call the night of Regan's birthday to find Regan next to her in her bed. Regan tells her mother that her bed was shaking. The next scene shows a priest putting flowers in front of holy statues on an altar. He turns from the statue of Joseph toward the Virgin Mary, and he sees the statue desecrated with protruding horns emerging from the breasts and genitalia. The timing of this scene is significant as it foreshadows the violation of Regan's own virginal body at the hands of the demon and the inability of her mother to protect her from the possession. The phallic horns on the statue also hint at the anxieties that will come with Regan's exorcism: the presence of the male demon distorting the female body, blurring the gender identity of the already-developing child's body. In perverting the image of the Virgin Mary, the film also perverts the idea of motherhood as sexual instead of sacred.

Chris loves her daughter, and her daughter loves her in return. Due to Chris's career, however, she is not able to spend as much time with Regan as her domestic role demands and instead relies on Karl and Sharon (Rudolph Schündler and Kitty Winn), her personal assistants, to act as caretakers for Regan in her absence. Regan shows a desire to not only spend more time with her mother but also to have a more nuclear-family unit.³ This is seen when Regan tells Chris that she can bring Burke Dennings (Jack MacGowran), Chris's romantic interest, with them to go see the sights on her birthday, resulting in the image of a family: mother, father, and child. Regan asks Chris if she is going to marry Burke to which Chris replies that she likes Burke but that he is merely a friend who comes around because he gets lonely. Some interpret this as jealousy on Regan's part toward Burke, with Regan viewing him as someone who will take her mother away from her. Penny Crofts argues: "The film could be read as explaining Regan's possession or rebellion as due to her desire to remain locked in a dyadic relationship with her mother. Regan's parents are divorced. She expresses jealous feelings toward Burke whom she thinks her mother wants to marry. Later, when she is possessed by the devil, Regan kills Burke" (20). Although Regan may wish to spend more time with her mother, the scene of Regan questioning her mother about Burke shows her desire for a father figure more than a desire for a closer relationship with her mother through the organization of her line of questioning, first asking if Chris loves him and then if she loved Regan's father. Pazuzu, in control of Regan's body, acts in response to Regan's desire for a father figure by killing and expelling rival male authorities from the house. Regan had hoped Burke would serve as a surrogate, earthly father figure, while Father Karras (Jason Miller) served as a stand-in for Regan's father in the end, sacrificing himself to save the daughter.

A neighboring scene shows Chris on the phone with the operator trying to get ahold of Regan's father on her birthday. Regan watches behind a wall across the hall, and her disappointment is clear. Because of this, Regan's possession can be seen as the demon responding to the instability of her family by her lewd sexual acts primarily directed toward male characters. It also shows the instability of her child body, with her in transition between girlhood and young adolescence. She recounts a day in the park with Sharon, saying, a "man came on a beautiful gray horse. . . . The guy let me ride it all around." The moment points to her desire for a father figure through the association of the horse with girlhood and the "guy" with a father. She describes her relationship with the imaginary Captain Howdy as one in which she asks the questions and he answers, a fabricated father-daughter relationship. His name alone notes his authority, with his fictional role as a "captain." She asks, "Do you think my mom is pretty?" Although the possessed Regan does kill Burke, his murder can be viewed as Pazuzu expelling the invasive male

Chris (Ellen Burstyn) lovingly looks at Regan (Linda Blair), asking the invisible Captain Howdy about her. © Warner Bros. Entertainment.

presence from the house so that his male authority remains intact while also further torturing Regan by taking away the possibility of a stable family unit. Crofts states this in saying, "Although it seems unjust that Regan is possessed, the film frees her and rewards her with a closer relationship with her mother. . . . The film exonerates her for her terrible deeds, but punishes the mother for wanting a new lover/husband and for disrupting her relationship with Regan. . . . She is forced back into her primary role as Mother. She is left with no lover and a scary daughter" (20). Chris struggled to sustain her motherly role to begin with, her maternity oftentimes conflicting with her public persona as an actress. What Chris is left with, then, is her ability to move forward with her life as the possession and subsequent exorcism act as warnings toward her maternal agency: that she must accept her role as mother to a pubescent daughter or lose her altogether.

Krzywinska comments on the relationship between Pazuzu, Regan, and Chris, saying: "Pazuzu works with Chris MacNeil's desire that Regan should remain a child. By prompting Regan to speak of sexuality, Pazuzu taps into MacNeil's fears of losing her daughter's innocent love" (248). Regan is taken to a doctor because of her erratic behavior. During examination, she displays unfeminine behavior. She lifts her skirt, showing her genitalia, shouting, "Fuck me! Fuck me!" to the medical staff. She swears at them, telling them to keep their fingers away from her "goddamn cunt," while the doctor first diagnoses her with a nerve disorder commonly seen in children her age. "Cunt" has a double meaning: referring to her genitalia and used as a derogatory term for a woman. Meanwhile, out in the waiting room, Chris knits an item with a giraffe on it. The parallel of these two images—Regan's examination and Chris's knitting—illustrates the friction between Chris's desire to infantilize her daughter and the reality of Regan's changing selfhood and body, both of which are dismissed by the predominantly male physicians who attempt to normalize Regan's clearly abnormal symptoms by writing them off with a blanket diagnosis common to individuals her age. The giraffe is also contrasted with the creatures Regan makes, which are combinations of different animals and similar to the Mesopotamian mythical creatures found in the same archeological dig that unearths the statue of Pazuzu.

Demonic Adolescence

Regan's violence toward others is largely sexual. She attacks the male doctors that try to treat her, attempting to overpower them. While under hypnosis, she admits that there is sometimes someone inside of her and attacks the doctor administering the hypnosis, grabbing his testicles before biting them through his clothing. The hypnosis reveals what her mother suspected: that Regan is not truly Regan, the daughter she thought she knew. Something has penetrated past the surface of her daughter's skin and, because of that, corrupted her sense of self. The demon has moved from the external house to the internal house of Regan's body. Claudia Benthien conceptualizes the body as a house, saying: "On one level, the windows of the body are understood to be exclusively the insular sensory organs concentrated on the skin (mouth, eyes, nose, ears). . . . On the second level, the circulatory exchange, with its acts of incorporation and excretion, is understood as entrance and exit movements in and out of the body-house, and the body orifices connected with this exchange are conceptualized as doors or gateways" (27). Regan verbally assaults Father Merrin (Max von Sydow) during the exorcism, calling him a "cock sucker" and telling him to "stick your cock up her ass, you motherfucking priest." Her verbal and physical attacks are meant to be shocking in contrast to her gendered female body, highlighting her Otherness and her disrupted body while also taunting the male authority.

The doctor's visit points to Chris's initial trust in the male-dominated medical community to cure her daughter of these troubling behaviors. The movement of the machines mimic that of her bed at home, trapping Regan inside of her possessed body and also representing the external possession of the demons of the patriarchal medical field. The doctor initially diagnoses Regan with a "disorder of the nerves, often seen in early adolescence. She has all the symptoms: hyperactivity, temper, performance of math." He prescribes Ritalin and cautions Chris: "Nobody knows the cause of hyperkinetic behavior in a child. Ritalin works to relieve the condition. As to how or why, we don't really know." This description is very similar to "hysteria," the medical term doctors used for centuries as a blanket diagnosis for women who displayed characteristics outside of societal norms. His diagnosis and treatment plan emphasize his cool, dismissive demeanor by focusing on the symptoms, the outward appearance, but not the underlying, deeper condition. His solution is no solution at all; instead, it is just a relief from her suffering. Despite Chris's questioning, Regan's mother accepts the doctor's authority when it comes to her daughter. In doing so, Chris chooses to forgo her maternal authority in favor of a paternal one. Because of this, she is able to resume her role as an actress. She throws a party at the house while Regan sleeps upstairs. Toward the end of the party, Regan comes downstairs, invading the parlor space and urinating on the carpet. Her forceful actions prompt Chris to go upstairs while still clad in her gown and give her daughter a sponge bath, bringing her back to her domestic role from her public one. Chris assures her daughter: "It's just like the doctor said. It's nerves. That's all. You just take your pills, and you'll be fine." Chris's acceptance of the doctor's treatment is not only to easily alleviate Regan's symptoms but also to alleviate Chris's stress so that she can continue her public life. Regan's urination is not the only spectacle of her abnormal body. She crawls downstairs and opens her mouth to reveal blood, signaling an opening of otherwise hidden orifices and entrances to the body.

Regan's symptoms only continue to get worse. Her bed violently shakes, leading her mother to return to the doctor's office for more tests. Dr. Klein's (Barton Heyman) diagnosis changes. He says: "It's symptom of the type of disturbance in chemical-electrical activity of the brain. In the case of your daughter, the temporal lobe on the left part of the brain. It's rare but it does cause hallucinations and usually just before convulsions. . . . The problem with your daughter is not the bed, it's the brain." His judgmental response dismisses Chris's claims that something else is happening and instead conclusively determines that her daughter is the problem. The solution is to surgically remove the scarring on the brain but only after tests can be done to confirm the diagnosis.

This treatment of Regan's body keeps with the patriarchal medical institution's historical practices of control and oppression toward women. Women's concerns and pain were often overlooked, neglected, and/or subject to torturous treatments. One such treatment was a lobotomy, a surgical procedure that involved damaging the brain. One of the primary reasons women were chosen for lobotomies was to correct deviant behavior: to do so limited their physical and cognitive agency and made them more controllable. Rather than examine the underlying cause of Regan's behavior, they enshrine her in the physical so that they can instead treat her symptoms and not the collective individual. Their solutions are more painful tests for her to undergo, such as spinal imaging, drugs, and removal of part of her brain. They refuse to turn to psychiatry to treat her, keeping with the antipsychiatry movement of the 1970s and with their focus on Regan's physical, not internal, self.[4] All the while, the doctors do not actually know what is wrong with her; they only know that her behavior is wrong for an adolescent girl to display.

Her symptoms eventually become such that they baffle the mostly male physicians consulted and escalate Chris's own frustration. The following dialogue takes place in which the doctors are forced to confront their confusion and failure to treat Regan:

DR. BARRINGER [Peter Masterson]: It looks like a type of disorder that you rarely ever see any more, except in primitive cultures. We call it a somnambular-form possession. Quite frankly, we don't know much about it, except that it starts with some conflict or guilt that eventually leads to the patient's delusion that his body's been invaded by an alien intelligence: a spirit, if you will.

CHRIS: Look, I'm telling you again, and you'd better believe it: I'm not about to put her in a goddamn asylum! And I don't care what you call it! I'm not putting her away!

BARRINGER: I'm sorry.

CHRIS: You're sorry! Jesus Christ, eighty-eight doctors, and all you can tell me with all of your bullshit is—

BARRINGER: There is one outside chance of a cure. I think of it as shock treatment. As I say, there is an outside chance . . . Have you ever heard of exorcism? It's a stylized ritual in which rabbis or priests try to drive out the

so-called invading spirit. It's pretty much discarded these days, except by
the Catholics who keep it in the closet as a sort of embarrassment. It has
worked, in fact, although not for the reason they think, of course. It was
purely the force of suggestion. The victim's belief in possession helped
cause it. And just in the same way, this belief in the power of exorcism can
make it disappear.

Regan typifies the deviant, uncontrollable woman the doctors imply
should be institutionalized for her behavior. Chris's insistence that she will
not put her daughter away and her anger toward Barringer highlights wom-
en's frustrations at the patriarchal healthcare system as Chris points out
their failure to adequately treat her daughter. Despite her reaction, Barringer
continues in a cold, matter-of-fact manner that casts Chris as the overly
emotional, irrational mother and Regan as the delusional female whose only
cure is an even greater delusion. Regan's symptoms are reduced to presumed,
projected beliefs on the part of the doctors; once again, the patient is blamed
and not the failure of the male dominated medical community. Chris's use
of "goddamn" and "Jesus Christ" have meanings that transcend her collo-
quial usage given that the context of the conversation is about her possessed
daughter. By invoking God with these terms, her language foreshadows that
the cure for Regan lies not with the paternal medical community, but with
a religious paternal authority.

Regan's physical, external body is emphasized during the religious intervention on her behalf, much as it was during the medical one. The power
of her body is illustrated in the notorious oral rape scene of her mother.
Intermingled with Regan's own cries for her mother is the demon's deep
voice, shouting, "May Jesus fuck you!" as Regan thrusts a silver crucifix
into her vagina. While this act may hint at a desire for a union with the
father figure through the choice of a crucifix, the spectacle of Regan forcing the phallic object into her vagina uses the symbolic male as merely a
tool in the sexual spectacle. The crucifix takes on added significance in the
scene since it is the object Regan and her mother struggle over, resulting
in Regan bringing her Chris's mouth to her genitalia, demanding, "Lick
me! Lick me!" and asserting her sexual dominance over her. The resulting blood reveals the physical harm inflicted on her body as well as being
symbolic of menstruation. She pauses, with her blood-splattered face, and
asks Chris, this time in Burke's voice, "Do you know what she did? Your

Regan's possession transforms her adolescence into a spectacle and turns her body into one that is abject. © Warner Bros. Entertainment.

cunting daughter?" The use of the three voices in the scene—Regan's and the two different male ones—demonstrates the shameful act she is forced to perform. The blood can also represent an inversion of transubstantiation whereby wine is converted into the blood of Christ. Here, it is both Regan's blood and that of the demon inside her, showing the interconnectedness of Regan and the demon.

Her innocence is robbed by the deep, overtly masculine voice that forces her into the act, while her shame is emphasized by the older voice whose questioning tone judges and condemns the act. The question's focus on Regan's genitalia contains her identity within her physical body, with the blood in the scene tied to stigma surrounding menstruation and the sexual female body. Before addressing Chris, Regan's head turns around backward as she sits on the bed with her legs spread open, crucifix in hand, ready to thrust it inside of her again. The movement of turning her head backward, away from the front of her body, to address her mother shows her turning away from the shameful act she just committed. The audience is meant to feel horror and sympathy for the two women in the scene—Chris and her daughter—as both are clearly violated and raped. Regan is once again rendered helpless against forces that are out of her control, a continuation of her prepossession state. Before, Regan was caught in the postdivorce fight between her mother and estranged father; now she is caught in the fight between holy and unholy forces.

The oral rape of her mother causes Chris to have a bloodstained mouth, similar to the blood staining Regan's genitals. The imagery is striking; not only is Chris brutally exposed to the realities of her daughter's adolescent body, but through being exposed to Regan's blood, Chris is forced to partake in a perversion of the sacrament of communion. Instead of accepting the symbolic blood of Christ, Chris is forced to accept the blood of possessed Regan, the symbolic act inverted so as to represent the sin of Regan's body:

> The individual's skin is burdened with shame in a special way when it is experienced as afflicted with blemishes and flaws. . . . On the level of visibility, the stigmatized skin shows the hidden, bad character; on the level of the sense of touch, it prevents any empathic contact that could eliminate this feeling of uncleanness and worthlessness. The skin imagined as repulsive forms a kind of blocade [sic] rendering impossible the touch that is both longed for and feared. A genuinely disfigured skin in, literally, such an encompassing stigma that the subject is not able to distance itself from this blemish. (Benthien 126)

The emphasis on her physical, sexual body points to the relationship between Chris and Regan: while Chris loves Regan, she is not able to be the traditional maternal archetype and chooses to view her daughter as cast in the role of an innocent child instead of a young woman. Through subverting the power of the mother, the holy order is subverted as well as the domestic. Chris is horrified by her daughter's acts and the subversion of her body, reaffirming her earlier statement that "that thing upstairs isn't my daughter."[5]

The overt sexual, physical, and spiritual tones in this scene highlight the concern surrounding Regan's possession. As Judith Butler states, "The boundary of the body as well as the distinction between internal and external is established through the ejection and transvaluation of something originally part of identity into a defiling otherness" (181–82). In forcing Regan to masturbate with a crucifix, Pazuzu can be seen as raping Regan, physically penetrating her vagina with the phallic crucifix. The force with which the possessed Regan thrusts the crucifix into her genitals and the resulting bleeding note an act of genital mutilation. Pazuzu physically breaks the boundary of Regan's body to further his corruption of it. Through the genital mutilation, the demon's possession can be interpreted as acting to take advantage of Regan's developing adolescent state so as to break the boundary of her body. In doing so, it can be read as Pazuzu claiming her body so that he can assert his dominance and manipulate the physical structure of the body. Pazuzu ensures that Regan is no longer a clean, innocent individual; rather, he sexually abuses her to control and dismantle her child identity.

The costuming of Regan's possessed body also points to her blurred gender identity through its connection with the performance of her gender identity. Butler writes, "Gender . . . serves as a unifying principle of the embodied self and maintains that unity over and against an 'opposite sex' whose structure is presumed to maintain a parallel but oppositional internal coherence among sex, gender, and desire" (30). During the aforementioned rape scene, Regan wears a white nightgown with a pale-pink checkered bodice that marks the purity and innocence that gets stained by the blood from the forced masturbation and mutilation. Later, a sedated, sleeping Regan wears a yellow button-down pajama set when Father Karras is called to witness the words "help me" etched into her abdomen from the inside. The choice of yellow is purposeful since it can connote both childhood and sickness. She wears a blue nightgown, however, when the actual exorcism takes place; the color is traditionally associated with men and is a fitting color to wear as the invasive male presence is exorcised from her body.

DECOMPOSITION AND RESTORATION

The violence of the scene clearly marks the declining state of Regan's physical body. Her skin whitens and grays. Her unkempt, unwashed hair frames her face, her eyes no longer look human, and she has dried, desiccated lips. She has yellow teeth, and open cuts and wounds line her face and body. By purposely cutting and slicing open parts of Regan's body, Pazuzu again alienates Regan's body from the normative female:

> The consistent pattern seems to be that the flayed woman is no longer a woman. Femaleness lies only in the dark and muddy breeding ground in the depths of the body or in the smooth and beautiful sheath-façade that surrounds this body but not in the powerful and vigorous, though profane, intervening layers of muscle and tissue. But woman is not surface *or* container. . . . The two notions, at least from the perspective of subconscious imagery, turn out to be two sides of the same conception: woman as hollow space with an enveloping, smooth external skin. (Benthien 89)

Her possessed body, in short, is a rotting body similar to that of, as Sara Cohen Shabot terms it, a meaty body: "The *meaty* body is indeed a perishing body, a body that can be corrupted, may get sick, and will ultimately die" (57, emphasis original). By visibly rotting her body, the demon transforms Regan from an individual to, simply, a flesh vessel. Doing so helps advance Pazuzu's ultimate goal: for Regan to die, to be his ultimate victim, a prize to be won.

As her possession ensues, her body becomes increasingly more grotesque, marking the union between the demon and herself. Her body is keeping with the theory of grotesque physicality, as Shabot states, "Grotesque bodies are hybrid bodies: mixtures of animals, objects, plants, and human beings." She characterizes them as "not clean, closed, well-defined, clear-cut, beautiful bodies striving for symmetry and order. Rather, the grotesque body is a body that defies clear definitions and borders and that occupies the middle ground between life and death" (Shabot 59). Shabot elaborates on the grotesque body in saying that the grotesque body is the excessive body. She notes, "The excesses of the body (and excesses in general) also constitute an important way of representing difference. The excess is that which has to be cleansed or eliminated when we try to overcome difference. . . . That which exceeds us, that which threatens our sameness, our 'normality,' our well-defined and protected presence in the world, constitutes the different" (Shabot 65). In possessing Regan, Pazuzu represents what must be cleansed from her: the unholy spirit. Doing so not only preserves the sanctity of Christianity but also reestablishes the order of the household by expelling the invasive male presence from the home. A nuclear-, holy-family model is put into place with the restoration of the child, earthly mother, and heavenly father.

The spectacle of Regan's possessed body forces Chris to eventually reach out to Regan's father, albeit a religious one, in the form of Father Karras and Father Merrin as well as the ultimate father, God.[6] Chris is not Christ, and it is the return of the father figure that saves Regan in the end, with Father Karras allowing the demon to enter his body, freeing both Regan and Chris from their turmoil. Father Merrin attempts to free the demon from Regan using the biblical exorcism. His failure to do so and subsequent death question the power of faith. It is this questioning of faith that occupies much of Father Karras's story in the film: unable to afford better care for his ailing mother, she passes away in a dilapidated, state-run hospital. Thus, in choosing to serve the Father he sacrifices his mother. His initial approach with Regan is also not a religious one; instead, he approaches her case from a psychological

The priestly fathers fight for Regan's soul. © Warner Bros. Entertainment.

perspective. Concerned that finishing the religious rite of exorcism would literally kill her, Father Karras cries, "Come into me! Goddamnit, take me!" before his medal of St. Joseph is ripped from his neck; thus, the holy father's body is made open to the unholy possession.[7] Struggling with the demon inside, Father Karras jumps from Regan's window to the base of the concrete stairs below, the imagery similar to that of Lucifer's fall from heaven that connotes the expulsion of the rebellious, evil spirit from the home. He dies, face down, on the concrete sidewalk, with his colleague scrambling to administer a final sacrament. His death is a complicated one: he saves Regan, but is he also saved?

The film restores balance to the family in reestablishing the bond between mother and child, while stabilizing the family with the return of the father, albeit a godly one. After the exorcism, Chris and Regan prepare to leave the Georgetown home and the events that happened there behind them, with white sheets covering the furniture, symbolically cleansing it before being moved to their next residence. The last image in the film is Regan's boarded-up window. Once used as a vessel of evil in committing murder, the opening of the house is now closed, sealing off the interior of the house from the exterior forces that threaten. In being freed from the demon, Regan's soul is once again sealed off from the demon. However, like many horror films, the film hints at a possible return with eerie music beginning to play while showcasing the boarded-up window. Just as the window can be reopened, so, too, could Regan's body.[8]

CHAPTER 3

The House Remembers
The Amityville Horror

Rosemary's Baby and *The Exorcist* each feature domestic dwellings that act as settings for the action that unfolds within. While these domestic spaces help to build onto the horror of what happens, they remain largely static as the characters move forward in the film. Such is not the case with *The Amityville Horror*. *The Amityville Horror* materializes the supernatural within the house itself, forcing the characters to confront their conflicting familial roles. As a result, the supernatural draws attention to Kathy's role as both wife and mother and, in the process, illustrates how those prescribed women's roles are not harmonious with one another.

The film begins with the fictionalized portrayal of the real-life murder of the DeFeo family where Ronald DeFeo Jr. murdered his parents and siblings with a shotgun before turning the gun on himself. These scenes are replayed as Kathy and George tour the house; as they open the door to each room, the film flashes back to the murder that took place in the room. The pairing of the scenes from the murder with George and Kathy's interest in the house likewise shows the overlap of the DeFeo and Lutz families.

"Houses don't have memories," George Lutz comments as he and Kathy tour the DeFeo murder house. George, Kathy, and their three children soon find out houses can have memories and that those memories can remind, fracture, and possess a family. Leftover furniture and mattresses remain in the rooms, and the real-estate agent makes a point of mentioning that if the Lutz's see any furniture that they would like that it can be included in the purchase of the home. Once moved in, viewers see that they took the real-estate agent up on the offer as the broken lamps and other furniture pieces are now utilized by the Lutz family. In doing so, the past, present, and future become intertwined with the Lutz's envisioning the potential for each room while foreshadowing the repetition of horror.

SATANIC PANIC

First released in 1979, the film can be considered part of the satanic panic that ensued in the 1980s, a phenomenon that was partly fueled by the onset of premium and basic cable as well as the VCR that allowed previous horror movies to enter the home (Beard 212). Beard writes, "Rendered more accessible than ever before, the supernatural horror movie of the late 1970s and early 1980s offered easily accessed and endlessly cycling visions of everyday life under attack from infernal forces capable of penetrating hearth and home in the age of Ronald Reagan and the late Cold War with the Soviet Union" (213). The film explores the tension between the secular and religious through grounding the narrative in a story involving two homes: the Amityville residential home and that of the church.

Richard A. Schoenherr and Lawrence A. Young find that while the number of priests grew from 1920 to 1965, it began to decrease after 1968 (465). Satanic panic resulted in a climate of fear and paranoia that satanic-cult members targeted and abused children. Just as evil was seen as entering residential homes during the 1980s, so too does the film make it seem that there is no escape from it, including in a house of God. In an argument with his fellow priests, Father Delaney (Rod Steiger) decries the "bureaucratic bullshit" of the church that he believes has led to his colleagues dismissing his call for action to help the Lutz family. Father Ryan's (Murray Hamilton) response echoes the Church's standpoint of the time, telling him, "We're not in the habit of blaming Satan for every phenomenon." Referencing the seemingly supernatural interference with the car on the way to the Lutz house, Father Ryan says, "I'd blame Detroit faster than the devil." His comment undermines his religious authority and his faith. The disillusionment of Father Ryan and the decision to relieve Father Delaney of his religious role connects with shifting patterns of priesthood during that time. Despite the lack of support from his fellow priests, Father Delaney continues in his attempts to help the Lutz's. He tries to call the house to warn Kathy, but a supernatural force blocks his call with static before choking him. Later, as he is giving a sermon at the altar of the church, he goes blind while uttering a prayer for God to give his parish "strength of mind and body!" His resulting blindness reads as punishment for his corporeal-motivated plea as much as the result of evil forces. Rather than strengthening his body, his blindness can be cause for introspection or a reflection on his faith.

SETTLING DOWN IN DEBT

In moving to the suburbs, Kathy and George inadvertently move into the devil's snare. Their consumerism and desire for the normalcy of a nuclear family, as opposed to the reality of their blended one, causes them to overlook the tragedy that took place in the home. Furniture remains from the previous, deceased homeowners, and some of it, in fact, remains in the home with the purchase. That the home is located in the suburbs, away from the city, on an expansive estate by the water, with a carriage house included, elevates the social standing of the family. More specifically, George's standing in the relationship is raised by securing his role as financial provider for his new family. Beard explains the danger of suburbia:

> Suburbia became its own trap while an increased awareness of domestic violence, child abuse and substance abuse called the institution of family into chilling question. Supernatural horror of the 1970s had offered filmgoers a new way of framing historically situated terrors and anxieties and the emergence of two key delivery systems, home video and cable television, allowed these films and newer supernatural horror films to haunt homes as never before, contributing to a social panic surrounding claims of satanic influence on everyday life, a panic that had been simmering in the United States since the late 1960s and throughout the 1970s. (216)

The Lutz's do not simply walk into suburbia's entrapment; rather, they welcome it with open arms. The audience does not know where they were living prior to the home but can deduce that it was a rental and therefore smaller and cheaper but more affordable. The home itself also stands out for its lack of these more commercial entertainment systems, home video and cable

George (James Brolin) and Kathy (Margot Kidder) talk about how to afford the home.
© American International Pictures.

television. Instead, the house itself and the supernatural provide distraction, entertainment, and danger for the family.

The home comes to represent economic mobility as well as mobility within the relationship. Kathy states, "We've always been a bunch of renters, and this is the first time, and this is the first time anyone has bought a house." Carol (Helen Shaver) comments that the house is "uptown" and is surprised by the size of it, saying, "I thought you guys owned a small business." Her remark shows the sharp economic contrast between the outward status the Lutz's attempt to portray with their home purchase and the underlying financial realities. Jeff (Michael Sacks) later informs George that the IRS has been contacting the office, employees have not been paid, and the business needs attention. The sign "Bless This Mess" stands above the kitchen sink, and the viewers see that the moving boxes are, in fact, old liquor boxes for whisky and brandy; this leftover packaging is used instead of purchasing new boxes.

Unfortunately for the Lutz's, no amount of repurposing will change the dark shadow that looms over and lives in their house. In its emphasis on the house as an entity, *The Amityville Horror* exemplifies the importance of home ownership in the horror genre. Tony Williams explains:

> Although the "Terrible House" often functions metaphorically as a Gothic motif in many horror films, it also has a specific economic basis. Home ownership, with its financial commitments and social obligations, is a fundamen-

tal component of capitalist society. The home anchors individuals within the system. Overburdening owners with high mortgage payments and property renovation, the home acts as an entrapment, ensuring that its victims comply with capitalism's maintenance. Salaries, wages, interest rates, desire for economic success, and continuing employment are all interrelated. (169)

Although their home is the symbolic "Terrible House," they remain tied to it out of financial circumstances even as the house continues to reject them. Kathy's aunt, Sister Helena (Irene Dailey), arrives at the house to face such rejection from the residence. Before her visit, black liquid spouts up from the toilets, keeping Kathy and George from greeting her. The mysterious liquid connects the house to the idea of a physical body, with the gurgling black liquid like decomposed flesh. She suddenly does not feel well in the home. Kathy pleads with her to stay and rest in the home. Kathy is shown as seeking approval from her family both in the home and her new life. The outfit she wears on the day of her nun aunt's visit is an imitation of a Catholic school girl. She makes a point of telling her aunt that she bought her favorite tea.[1] Still, her aunt leaves the house. Once a safe distance away from the house, she retches and vomits. The parallel between these details points to the association with the house and disease. Despite the attempt to organize and define the home into a space that is their own, the Lutz's are a symbolic "mess," much like the sign hanging above the sink says. They are a blended family living in a haunted house whose supernatural events escalate already-existing tensions and possess George, the surrogate, symbolic father figure. The black liquid bubbling up from the toilet signifies the decay of the home and that of the family's emotional and financial stability; much as they try to push aside what happened, as the events unfold, the house makes it clearer and clearer that it will resurface.

For George and Kathy, owning a home together marks a turning point in their relationship. The real-estate agent notes that the home would be great for a big family; however, George clarifies that they already have a family with three young children. The children belong to Kathy from a previous relationship. Her economic background shapes much of the film and gives insight into her socioeconomic status since "single motherhood grew rapidly during the 1970s, when the number of families with children headed by single mothers increased 83%. The growth rate slowed to 35% in the 1980s and to 15% in the 1990s" (Johnson and Favreault S315). Not only did single motherhood

increase, so too did the number of households headed by women: "The pro-
portion of all families in the United States headed by women has increased
dramatically in recent decades, increasing from 7.4% in 1960 to 23.2% in
1985," according to the US Bureau of the Census (Johnson and Favreault
S315). Richard W. Johnson and Melissa M. Favreault demonstrate the limited
socioeconomic opportunities available to single women with children:

> Before welfare reform began in the 1990s, the existence of welfare benefits
> reduced the benefits of work. Single women with dependent children could
> qualify for public support if they were not employed, and they would lose their
> benefits if they did work and earned much income. As a result, employment rates
> among single mothers were low. Those who do work tend to earn low wages,
> because they generally have little education and limited experience. (S316)

She admits to George, "I want this to work. . . . I don't want you to have
regrets." This admission points to an acknowledgement of her socioeconomic circumstances as a single mother with three children married
to an otherwise eligible bachelor. Her desire to keep George satisfied in the
relationship can thus be seen as more than just for emotional reasons but
for economic ones as well.

The house quickly becomes a source of strife between George and Kathy.
She pleads with him to notice that the family might be in danger in the
house. He slaps her, telling her: "I'm not going anywhere. You're the one
who wanted a house, so just shut up!" In placing the desire for the home
on Kathy, he associates any fault with the home with her. He demands that
she stop "nagging" him about her concerns and passive-aggressively implies
his dissatisfaction with the lack of progress made unpacking boxes—all of
which is somehow her fault.

WIFE VS. MOTHER

Home ownership heightens the duality of Kathy's role as wife to George and
mother of her children. The day of her brother's wedding, George snaps at
Kathy about the noise the children are making outside. When they come
home that night to find a crying babysitter locked in Amy's (Natasha Ryan)
closet, he is astounded at Amy's passive demeanor about listening to the

babysitter's pleas for help for hours while the boys gawk from the doorway. He tells Kathy, "These kids of yours need some goddamn discipline." In that moment, it becomes clear that Kathy is responsible for keeping the children—her children—from troubling George or anyone else, thus detaching George from the paternal role. It also becomes clear that Kathy's mechanisms for handling both her roles involve pacifying George through sex and a passive attitude toward her children.

The film presents a complicated view of maternity. The symbolic maternal of the church is shown as ultimately failing to protect its members and priests as the house targets those attempting to call upon the faith. Statues of the Virgin Mary appear throughout in both the church and in the Lutz's home. Kathy even begins to paint a white statue of the Virgin. On the one hand, this can be seen as her appealing to the Virgin's power in her attention to the iconography; on the other hand, it can also be read as Kathy attempting to navigate issues of motherhood that present her at odds with being both the good mother to her children and exercising sexual agency in her relationship with George. She eyes her body in the bedroom mirror before sex, initiates physical intimacy with George, and turns to her reflection during intercourse.

The sexually intimate scene is interrupted by Amy, Kathy's daughter. She cries, "I want to go home," and Kathy puts the child back to bed wearing George's shirt. The action casts Kathy as a mimic of George. Her movements likewise mirror George from when he tucked Amy in as she closes the same window George closed when he put Amy to bed the first time. After she leaves, the rocking chair begins moving on its own. The significance of the parent wearing the shirt posits the wearer in an authority role, with George representing familial security and Kathy, emotional stability. Although George is the one who initially puts the child to bed, Kathy is the one who reassures her. This repetitive action between George and Kathy shows Kathy as not her own person; she copies George, imitating him.

George later remarks that couples have had to live with children interrupting their intimacy "since Adam and Eve got kicked out of the Garden. Just have to learn to live with it." His words are significant and imply that their relations are forbidden as their physical relationship is for pleasure and not reproductive reasons. She grabs George from behind as he chops wood, and he warns her, "don't ever do that, not to a man with an axe in his hand." In both scenes, her sexual desire is policed: first by Amy and then by George. George's comment likewise shows the underlying sexual tension that helps

The first time we see Kathy after buying the house. © American International Pictures.

enable the possession, with Kathy's sexual initiation seen as a challenge to his symbolic masculinity.

She calls George a "regular daddy" because of his concern for the children playing too close to the river. Because of the costuming of her character—dressed in tight-fitting jeans and hair in pigtails—the line can also be read as sexual. Alone in the bedroom that night, she puts a daisy in her hair, adorning herself with a symbol of virginal maidenhood. She is clad in all white—underwear, shirt, and leg warmers—and performs a pirouette in front of the mirror that shows off her cleavage and form. George surprises her in the doorway as we see the outline of her breast. The scene posits George in a predatory position, viewing the unknowing Kathy, who symbolizes innocence in all white and by mimicking a ballerina, a role typically associated with girl-hood. Toward the end of the film, this sexualized costuming decreases as she is instead shown wearing long nightgowns, layered sweaters, and long skirts. This all correlates to her detachment from George as he becomes increasingly distanced in their relationship. He lays with his back turned away from her in bed. She says, "George, I have to talk to you," but he ignores her.

Her complicated motherhood and marriage are also shown in the fetishization of her body. When we first see her, her outfit is not sexualized. She wears a white turtleneck and beige overcoat. This soon changes as she is costumed in increasingly sexualized outfits. She wears a plaid skirt and white blouse with a folded sweater over her shoulders to get groceries. The outfit is complete with a faux tie and knee-high socks, reminiscent of a Catholic

The increased fetishization of Kathy. © American International Pictures.

school girl. When unpacking the house, she is shown in pigtails with plaid ribbons in her hair that match the pattern on George's shirt. The pigtails paired with the white shirt create a girlish appearance, shown as she puts liner paper on the shelves. The top button is unbuttoned so that, when she bends over, the viewer sees her cleavage and a cross.

POSSESSED PATERNAL

The instability of the family structure fuels George's possession by challenging his role in the home and family. With the move to a new house, George hopes for the children to look to him as a father figure. He makes this clear as they are moving in, telling Kathy he might feel like a father if the children started addressing him as such "instead of George, which I got to admit is better than all that Mr. Lutz crap." His comment highlights the tension in the relationship: George is seen as the outside masculine influence, not fully accepted into the familial unit. In addition, the film makes it clear that the move has cost him financially. The house draws on this financial insecurity as part of George's possession. George writes a personal check to cover the catering for his brother-in-law's wedding after the money mysteriously disappears. He searches the house for the money only to find an empty money band. The check he wrote subsequently bounces, leading him into further financial debt.

George's possession most impacts his relationship with Kathy and the children through questioning his masculine role as provider. He wakes up every morning at 3:15 a.m., the same time that the DeFeo murders occurred and a time that represents the inversion of the trinity. He hears voices and gunshots in the house. When he goes downstairs to investigate, he wears nothing but a shirt and underwear, exposing his legs and showing him as physically vulnerable. He hears flies and sees the fly-infested room. The front door slams open and breaks off the hinges, alerting Kathy to the sound. The basement door is also blown off the hinges. When they go upstairs, the previously fly-infested room is now devoid of insects. The police detective determines that the door was broken from the inside, not the outside, implying that the invasive force came from inside the house, not outside. The scene is important because it questions whether the occurrences are due to a supernatural element or are a product of George's pent-up aggression.

His possession is initially marked by an obsession with maintaining the home through checking on a light from the boathouse and chopping wood to supply heat. At one point he cries, "What do you want from us? Goddamn it, this is my house!" As the possession increasingly takes hold, he undergoes physical and emotional changes. His hair and beard grow longer and shaggier, transforming his appearance to that of Ronald DeFeo. His possession thus becomes his transformation into a double, or doppelganger, of DeFeo. Freud explains the concept of the double in relation to the individual self: "A person may identify himself with another and so become unsure of his true self; or he may substitute the other's self for his own. The self may thus be duplicated, divided and interchanged. Finally, there is the constant recurrence of the same thing, the repetition of the same facial features, the same characters, the same destinies, the same misdeeds, even the same names, through successive generations" (142). His outward hypermasculinity corresponds to sexual dysfunction. Unlike the first intimate scene, the viewer is not privy to the overly sensualized movement and costuming. Kathy lights a cigarette in bed, laying next to a shirtless George. She reassures him: "This sort of thing happens all the time. You don't have to prove anything to me." He replies: "I'm sorry. I don't know what's wrong with me," connoting his embarrassment and the connection between his sexual and internal self. As the possession takes increased hold on him, he obsessively chops wood and sharpens his axe, the symbolic phallus. He patronizes Kathy for her lack of discipline with the children. His behavior escalates to physical and verbal abuse toward Kathy.

Through his possession, he is also sexualized. He only wears jeans and a jacket, no shirt, to go investigate the light in the boathouse in the early morning hours. He is visibly sweaty as he chops wood for the home. In sexualizing George, the film likewise undermines his role as a patriarchal authority: "The repressed is patriarchal hatred, fear, and self-loathing. As the culture changes, as patriarchy is challenged, as more and more families no longer conform in structure, membership, and behavior to the standards set by bourgeois mythology, the horror film plays out the rage of paternal responsibility denied the economic and political benefits of patriarchal power" (Sobchack 180). He struggles in his role as the financial provider for the family, unable to find the money Kathy's brother set aside to pay the caterer on their wedding day. In turn, he is forced to write a check that bounces. As he struggles to find his place in the home, his business struggles as well. To compensate for these insecurities, he displays hypermasculinity. He rides a motorcycle and steals a library book by putting it down his pants. He snaps at Kathy, physically assaulting her by slapping her. The soft-spoken, caring, easy-going George from the beginning of the film is no more.

The more George spirals into possession, the more he increasingly demonstrates traditional masculine traits. As Vivian Sobchack writes, "*The Amityville Horror* is figured not only as the haunted middle-class family home, but also as the haunted middle-class family Dad—who, weak, economically beleaguered, and under pressure from his corrupt and demanding dream house in a period of economic recession, terrorizes his children" (180). He enters the home with an axe, looking for the children. As he goes from room to room, he cannot find the children until he realizes they are in the bathroom in the attic. He tries to break into the room with the axe, but Kathy grabs him from behind. She turns just in time to avoid George's axe and cries, "Don't hurt my babies." It is this plea that breaks the possession on George. In doing so, it is Kathy's power of maternity that overpowers that of the hypermasculine possession through reminding both George and the house of her role as a mother.

The house, however, is not the only force influencing George. His friend Jeff also contributes to George's hypermasculinity through his role as George's business partner. He taunts George, remarking: "The business is falling apart. People are calling. Bills have to be paid. I know you're busy unpacking, but life goes on." Jeff's comment is very dismissive of George's domestic life and shows the divide between the domestic and professional when it comes to masculinity. He purposely insults George's marriage to Kathy in saying: "I told you you were taking on too much. You marry a dame with three kids, you buy a big house with mortgages up to your ass, you change your religion, and you forget about business." George's response is to punch him, an action that pleases Jeff because it allows him to control George, asking him, "Now can we talk?" Jeff resorts to provoking violence from George in order to get his attention, associating violence with action; doing so shows George's reversion to traditional masculinity. Jeff's solution likewise shows this emphasis on traditional modes of manhood. The structure of the dialogue points to the connection between the failing business and George's marriage to a single mother. Kathy is seen as a drain on the business as well as a force that changes George and not for the better.

George's possession and role in the family comes to a head in the climax of the film during which Kathy's maternity is most highlighted.[2] It is here that she is seen as protecting her children from the outside forces. Before this, she is most concerned with pleasing and attending to George to keep him sexually, emotionally, and physically satisfied with her and the marriage. She experiences a dream in which she sees George kill Amy with an axe before turning it on her and decides to investigate the DeFeo murders. It is then that she realizes that George has fully transformed into a double of DeFeo, and she hides her children from the anticipated attempted murders that would mimic the DeFeo murders. Ronald DeFeo Jr. shot his family in the head, execution style, with a shotgun—a murder method that represents hypermasculinity.

THE HOUSE AND FAMILY DIVIDED

As this takes place, the house bleeds from the walls and the stairs, an act that feminizes the house through associations with menstruation. In bleeding blood, the house shows itself as alive and fertile. It is no longer spewing black bile from the toilets; it is now an active agent in expelling the Lutz's from its domain. The feminization of the home is first shown through the penetrative act whereby George takes a pickaxe to the stone wall in the basement. Carol claims that behind that wall is where the mentally ill were housed and abandoned to die, marking it as an abject space. As George breaks through with the pickaxe, the red that splashes the stone is exposed to create a vaginal effect.

Red is repeated throughout the film with the symbolism of blood and disease. The red of the secret room corresponds to the opening horizon of the film, with the red sky and black trees and outline of the house, shrouding it in an atmosphere of evil. As the credits progress, the horizon becomes noticeably lighter, fading to a gray. The scene is then cut with steady images of rainfall and a storm that shows the exterior. This is the night of the DeFeo murder, the sounds of the gunshots mingling with that of thunder. The scene creates a symbolic baptism of the house, forever steeping it in a history of evil. When Father Delaney attempts to bless the house from the upstairs room, a closeup of the eyes of the swarming flies show them as red. The shape of the eyes is similar to that of the windows of the home, representing the home as diseased and infected.[3]

It is not only the corporeal religious aspects that are undermined but also the symbolic religious ones. During his possession, George wails, "I'm coming apart! Oh, Mother of God, I'm coming apart!" As George and Kathy attempt to bless the house themselves, going from room to room with a silver crucifix, George's hand burns from the metal, while Kathy's face blisters. She stares at her reflection in the same mirror where she initiated sex earlier and tells George, "Don't look at me." Her reaction undermines her faith in her marriage to George by associating her value to him as physical. Kathy calls Father Delaney for help, crying "Father! Father!" into the phone; yet the line gets unexpectedly cut short. She tries to say the Lord's Prayer but is unable to finish. The house's interference with father figures—paternal George and religious Father Delaney—further puts the family in danger and urges Kathy to intervene on the family's behalf to save it.

The relationship between the house and disease is again seen through Father Delaney's demise. Originally called to bless the house, he enters an empty home while the family plays outside. He hears the sound of giggling children upstairs, but no one is in the room, except a statue of the Virgin Mary in the corner. Despite trying to open the window due to a sudden spike in the room's temperature, the window will not open. As he recites the blessing of the house, black flies accumulate on both the outside and inside of the closed window. He experiences a coughing fit and hears a voice distinctly command him to "Get out!" in response to his own command that there be "God's peace in this house." He finally leaves the home, and as soon as he is outside, he can breathe again. Even with a physical statue of the Virgin Mary and his faith, he fails to bless the house and expel the evil.

Father Delaney attempts to gain support from his fellow priests in order to intervene on the Lutz's behalf, feeling that they are in danger while they stay in the home. He is dismissed, however, as Father Ryan (Murray Hamilton) states: "You haven't told us one thing that can't be written off as simple hysteria. Even psychotherapists lose touch with reality sometimes. Your education doesn't give you any immunity." Father Ryan's words demasculinize Father Delaney, diagnosing his symptoms as hysteria, a condition traditionally associated with women. Father Delaney's response furthers his feminization, saying: "To me, the church is my home. The church is my strength, and I need her now, and that family needs her." He begins to cry. His emotional plea undermines his masculine authority by saying he needs the female-personified church and by his show of emotion. And what was the solution proposed by the other priests? For Father Delaney to take a vacation and see his family.

No longer recognized by his peers as part of the church family, Father Delaney is prescribed the same dismissive treatment many women diagnosed with hysteria were given: to rest and let the problems go away on their own. Father Nuncio states his belief that "we create our own demons in our own mind." Father Delaney is not only abandoned by his fellow priests, brothers in faith as well as colleagues, but also by religion itself. He prays for God to "give them [parishioners] health of mind and body. . . . Give them strength of mind and body." He feverishly repeats this prayer and focuses his attention on one of the angelic images lining the ceiling. As he continues in prayer, he imagines the face of the angel crumbling and falling toward him. He shields his face from the perceived attack only to come to the reality that the church building is still intact. The incident, however, renders him blind as he is failed by the church and his faith.

The Amityville Horror takes issues of home ownership and transforms them into a narrative about economic and familial instability. At the end, the Lutz's simply leave the home and relocate to another state. The house remains unchanged and unaffected, while the family is forever changed. We do not know what happens to the family after leaving the home. Instead, we know that the house stands, and the family runs, emotionally scattered, into the night outside.

HAUNTED KIDS IN HAUNTED HOUSES

Because the parents' relationship is unstable, the children are influenced by the home as well. Amy, Kathy's youngest child and only daughter, shows changes in behavior and attitude. Kathy states that the reason why Amy does not attend the wedding is because she has a virus, but Amy later tells the babysitter: "I wasn't sick. I just didn't like the meatloaf." When her babysitter becomes locked in the closet and cries for Amy to open the door, Amy remains on the bed unmoved, staring at the closet door as the babysitter frantically knocks on door. She tells her parents that Jodi would not let her unlock the door and is yelled at by George. She says, "George yelled at me" yet remains unmoved both in body and voice as she says so. She adds, "Jodi doesn't like George." Amy plays disciplinarian with her dolls, telling one to "quit being a smartass," a phrase that makes the viewer question whether she overheard it from her parents or from Jodi. A window slams shut on her brother's hand as he teases her from a room above.[4] Amy is the only one able to see Jodi and writes her name on the wall toward the end of the film when the hauntings and possession escalates. She draws the *o* in Jodi's name in red, with an effect similar to that of a portal.

It is never clear who Jodi is. The only insight provided is when Amy relays to Kathy that "Jodi's nice. . . . She tells me about the little boy who used to live in our room. . . . She says she wants me to live here forever and ever so that we can all play together." While the house acts to entertain Amy, it primarily targets men in its attack. Similarly, Kathy uses an upstairs room for her painting without incident, whereas the men come under assault. Kathy's art room is the same room George sees as being infested with flies before flashing to show that it is empty, where flies swarmed around Father Delaney, and the one in which a window lands on Billy's hand as he and his brother tease Amy. The latter action happens after Kathy asks, "What are you two rascals doing in my room?"

The Amityville Horror is certainly not the first haunted house film; that credit belongs to the 1927 silent movie *The Cat and the Canary*. Yet it is the first haunted house to focus on a nuclear family. In doing so, it helped pave the way for the haunted-house movies that followed. *The Shining* (1980), *Poltergeist* (1982), and *Beetlejuice* (1988) are all haunted-house films with one commonality: they center on families that move into homes that are already occupied by the supernatural. *The Amityville Horror* also acts as the predecessor for more contemporary horror films, including the *Insidious* and *The Conjuring* franchises, which will be explored in the next chapters.

CHAPTER 4

Danger All Around
Insidious and *Insidious: Chapter 2*

While it was the house that haunted in *The Amityville Horror*, the hauntings that occur in the *Insidious* films result from the suppressed supernatural. The actual house is both tangible and abstract, with the image of the house shown as one that can be located inside of the self as well as around it.[1] As opposed to other possession films, in this one, a house itself is not haunted; rather, it is an individual who is haunted. Dewey Musante notes this:

> In *Insidious*, it is not the house that suffers from a demonic presence and roaming human spirits, but the body itself. Not just a body, but all bodies; those alive and dead, moving and still, believing and non-believing and, most importantly, those in the film and those viewing it. The ghosts in *Insidious* break from the confines of the typical haunted house film and are no longer tied to the physical structure of the house, but merge with the rhythm of the film. Haunting, then, is thrown into chaos. Ghosts are not tied to an old locket, a dusty basement or a creaking attic; they are tied to the body, specifically, a body that they have never inhabited. In this sense, the true horror of *Insidious* is not the ghost or demon suddenly appearing in the frame or the uncanny weirdness of an old house, but the eerie supposition that our bodies are not tied even to our souls; that the body itself is uncanny. (74)

To be haunted is shown as a patrilineal characteristic with the character Josh passing on the ability of astral projection to his son Dalton. This power causes Dalton to drift too far into another dimension, known as the Further, and, in doing so, invites spirits into physical reality, spirits who then attempts to possess his corporeal body while his astral self is locked away. Bringing Dalton back from this place involves Josh calling on his own repressed abilities to journey into the Further. In doing so, the ghosts are presented as posttraumatic stress that Josh is forced to confront. *Insidious* and the sequel, *Insidious: Chapter 2*, explore the relationships between physical and psychic bodies to expose the intersection of parenting, possession, and trauma.

The opening scene of the first film underpins this overlap and overviews the underlying conflict in the first and second films. A young Josh is shown sleeping from a distance before the camera moves to a silhouette of a ghostly woman outside of a window. Finally, the camera pauses as a woman in a black wedding dress stares into the center of the frame. Although this is the first scene of the first *Insidious* movie, it directly connects with *Insidious: Chapter 2* through revealing the antagonistic spirits responsible for adult Josh's possession and the central conflict in the second movie. Josh is not possessed in *Insidious* until the end; leading up to that, it is his son Dalton whose possession shapes much of the movie.

The audience, however, does not know this going into the first movie. In fact, *Insidious* and *Insidious: Chapter 2* make it a point to keep the audience unaware of the many connections between the pair until viewers have seen both films. Musante comments on this, remarking, "Removed from narrative thrust or visual figurations of the typical film action, this opening sequence presents us with a rendering visible of the 'insidious' and uncanny concept of corporeality" (81). The mysterious knocking on the front door and security alarm that stirs Josh to go downstairs and investigate in *Insidious* is revealed in *Insidious: Chapter 2* to not be caused by an unknown spirit but his own astral self who tries to alert the family to the threat of ghostly visitors attempting to possess their children.

After learning of the parasitic entities of Michelle (Danielle Bisutti), otherwise known as Mater Mortis, and the woman in black (Philip Friedman), the opening scene of *Insidious* can be seen as offering the audience clues to *Insidious: Chapter 2*'s plot. Michelle, always shown in white, abused her son and forced him to adopt a woman's identity. In adulthood, he became a serial killer known as the woman in black, who was haunted by his mother's toxic spirit. The woman in black became the spirit who attempted to possess a young Josh and later succeeded in possessing his adult body; as a result, he was not only possessed by the woman in black but also by Michelle.

The effect this lack of knowing causes is to destabilize the narrative. The audience does not know anything the movie does not tell them. In doing so, the films invite the viewer to experience the hauntings and possession as the characters themselves experience it. This adds to the terror and increases the threat level of the supernatural by being unable to provide context for its existence. Ghosts such as the one who attacks Renai and the very demon of *Insidious* who nearly fully possesses Dalton are given vague descriptors instead of names, with the credits attributing those actors to the parts of "Long Haired Fiend" and "Lipstick-Face Demon." The lack of definition is meant to unsettle. These are not simply individual spirits targeting the Lambert family; rather, the spirits in the movie are just a few of the many that live in a realm adjacent to physical reality. *Insidious* and *Insidious: Chapter 2* make this distinction clear through the patrilineal ability to astral project into the psychic dimension, dividing the physical and inner self to disrupt the idea of a composed body.

THE SHARED SELF

The first movie introduces viewers to the Lambert family and their transition in moving into a new house.[2] The audience is never told where they moved from or why they moved. The only possible explanation is implied in a comment Renai makes to Josh when she says, "I want this house to be different" and when she later remarks, "I'm scared nothing is going to change." It is unclear how it is supposed to be different since we are never provided with the knowledge of what came before. What we are provided with are Renai's struggles to control the space and the family as it is made clear that she is responsible for structuring the physical home through unpacking and arranging items, as well as maintaining the familial structure of the internal homelife. She is the first to wake while Josh sleeps in. Adorned in pajamas with cartoonish monkeys on them, she quietly descends into the living room to put books away and revisit family memories in photo albums. She looks at a picture of when she and her husband, Josh, were married, foreshadowing the end of wedded bliss that follows. Dalton soon joins her, wearing matching pajamas. The mother and son sit together revisiting the photo album;

Renai (Rose Byrne) shares her space and selfhood with son Dalton (Ty Simpkins). © Sony Pictures.

together, they almost look as one to make clear that Renai's self is directly tied to her children. The album not only includes photos of the couple as husband and wife and father and mother but also individual photos of Renai before she was married; thus, it acts to show the transformation of Renai from an individual self into a shared self. It also introduces the theme of erasure of one's personal identity. Dalton's observation that there are no photos of Josh in the album from when he was younger likewise echoes Renai's tie to the family as does the cry of baby Kali who harkens the start of the day and diverts his mother's attention elsewhere.

Not only does Renai share her selfhood with her children but also with Josh. The quiet moment with the photo album is sharply contrasted with that of the tiny, cramped kitchen and breakfast. She stands frustrated as she, attempting to change the family's phone number, repeatedly demands on the phone, "Speak to an agent." As she does this, she intervenes between Dalton and Foster (Andrew Astor), who fight over a cereal bowl. She stands next to the stove, placing her in a centralized location in the space to emphasize her exasperated role in the domestic. When Foster criticizes her for giving him a large mug for cereal, saying that it is too small, she tells him, "Just make it work!" In addition to taking care of the children and financial issues, she also ties Josh's tie. Despite these motions, she never actually moves in the kitchen; instead, she stays mostly fixed in the middle. She is also unable to challenge Josh's seeming inability to assist with dropping off and picking up the boys from school as he leaves her stationary and voiceless. She is thus constantly attached to the domestic and the house, denied the ability to move beyond that. This characteristic is later echoed in the fact that Josh, not her, possesses the ability to move beyond the physical home into the projected, astral one.

The concept of Renai's shared selfhood is one that the film also explores through her music. The book shown on the shelf is *Self-Healing through Music*, a title that offers potential insight into the pain Renai harbors. After the chaos of breakfast, she sits at the piano and writes a song, singing: "I'm gonna be somebody. I just can't be her today." But she is again interrupted by the baby crying, tearing her away from an action that would be self-care. The song notes longing to be an individual other than oneself and offers insight into Renai's inner self: that she is conscious of her shared selfhood and, while she accepts it, is not satisfied being just a wife and mother. Later that night, Josh asks Renai if she needs help putting boxes away upstairs. His question comes at the end of the day while the pair are getting ready for bed, rendering the offer a moot point. He walks away, as he puts moisturizer around his eyes, saying, "I just hate feeling helpless." He, however, is not the helpless parent; as Renai explains, she tried to get work done but was forced to take care of Kali instead and, as a result, had to focus on her role as a mother instead of herself.

When she realizes that her sheet music has gone missing, it is Dalton, not Josh, who climbs to the attic to find it; he dons a superhero cape to do it, an outfit choice that rewards his active response. Dalton gets injured in the process, falling off a broken ladder.[3] Josh comes to his son's aide, carrying him in his arms. This scene will later act as to foreshadow Dalton's entrapment in the Further, with the positioning of his body in the attic similar to that in the demon's lair; both times, it is the father who is called to action.

TECHNOLOGY AND THE SUPERNATURAL

Renai is also the parent who experiences and documents the supernatural in the home through her interaction with medical technology. The film shows Renai as the parent present for the home healthcare nurse to show how to take care of Dalton, including how to insert the feeding tube and change his IV. Because she is the sole parent responsible for Dalton's medical needs, she is able to spot a bloodied red claw print near Dalton's foot. She alerts Josh of her discovery, but he rebuffs her insistence that they should be alarmed:

RENAI: Josh, I'm scared. I'm so scared, and I—

JOSH: I'm scared. He's my son, too.

RENAI: You don't understand. I'm scared for Dalton. I'm scared of this house.
There's something wrong with this place. I'm not imagining it. I can feel
it. It's . . . it's like a sickness. Ever since we moved in, everything's just gone
wrong.

JOSH: You think our house is haunted?

RENAI: I don't think it. I know it. Things move around in here by themselves. I
walk into the kitchen at night and can feel eyes on me . . . I can't be in there
alone anymore. I need you. You're never here. Where are you?

JOSH: I told you. I was grading tests.

RENAI: That's not what I mean. You're not here with me, in this situation.
You're just avoiding it. Like everything that's stressful, whether it's this or
parking tickets or—

JOSH: Stop saying that. I don't avoid stressful situations. Just dealing with
them in my own fucking way.

RENAI: Fine. [Throws sheet at him.]

Renai describes the house as a "sickness," associating Dalton's medical
situation with the house. She holds Josh accountable for his absence from the
home as an avoidance of stressful situations; in doing so, Josh's character is
shown as immature, which undermines his masculinity. Josh's lack of place
in the home can also be connected to his refusal to acknowledge events that
are beyond his control. Even when he accepts that there are spirits entering
the home and targeting his family, he tells his wife: "I do believe you. I just
don't know what you want me to do." He once again remains passive against
the active threat to this family; the more passive he remains, the more the
threat looms. This later becomes parallel to Josh's childhood, when he was
helpless against the supernatural and needing his mother to intervene. Here,
he relies on Renai as the mother figure to take on that responsibility.

The overlap between technology and the supernatural in the film is a
common element in many horror films. Murphy comments on the role
of technology in horror films and *Insidious*, saying, "As is usually the case
in haunted house narratives more generally, technology—be it recording
equipment or otherwise—is always associated with male characters" (239).
Although she points out that in *Insidious*, psychic Elise Rainier's (Lin Shaye)
assistants, Specs and Tucker (Leigh Whannell and Angus Sampson), handle

Elise (Lin Shaye) protects herself before communicating with spirits. © Sony Pictures.

the technology equipment, the baby monitor can be considered a piece of technology that is maternal. Murphy further explains the traditional connection between technology and the masculine:

> What the presence of technology wielded by male characters also does here is affirm the impossibility of trying to record, control, or expel malevolent supernatural forces in any strictly "rational" manner (one could reasonably object to this problematic suggestion that rationality is a specifically masculine trait, but it should be pointed out that in all of these films, the urge to "document" or engage with the supernatural also backfires upon the men concerned). (240)

Insidious subverts this tradition through the significance of the baby monitor. Because of her role as a stay-at-home mother, Renai is the one who wields the technology that alerts her to supernatural occurrences. She overhears a voice on the baby monitor, whispering: "I want it. I want it now!" She also reacts and responds to the baby's cries, which often harken the presence of a spirit. Because she gave birth to Kali, Kali can also be read as an extension of Renai's reproductive technology and of Renai herself. Kali's name carries with it the association to the Hindu goddess Kali, who is depicted as a protector against evil and whose name can also be interpreted to have meanings associated with time itself.

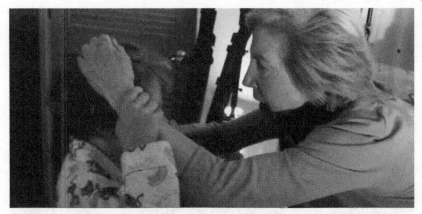

Elise, as an unconventional exorcist, temporarily expels the demon's control over Dalton.
© Sony Pictures.

The intersection between technology and the supernatural continues during a séance. Elise wears a gas mask during it. The gas mask is typically seen as a protective device designed to filter out noxious particles. For her to then wear it during a séance posits the supernatural as physically dangerous. She breathes heavily as the beeping of Dalton's heart monitor is heard in the background. During the séance, a possessed Dalton appears at the table, rips the room apart, and spirits surround the family. Elise grabs Dalton by the head and commands the possessing spirit to "leave this vessel!" And she turns on the light to dispel the dead. When reviewing camera footage from the séance, it is revealed that the demon was controlling Dalton's catatonic body like a puppet.

PARENTING STYLES

Because Josh is unable to resolve the situation, Renai must make the executive decision to move the family in an effort to get away from the hauntings; to her, ghosts haunt houses. They move into a rental home with near identical landscaping to their former home, bringing into question how different the domestic situation will be in their new residence. Very soon into the move, Renai realizes that the house is very much the same as their other one as she begins to witness spirits freely roaming the rooms. Strange music plays, spirits appear, doors shut on their own, and Renai has this startling realization:

"This thing from the other house has followed us here." The family later finds Dalton's room in chaos as objects and furniture have been thrown about. Renai pleads with Josh, "Please, please help him." Just as before, however, it is not Josh who helps solve the pressing problem; it is instead his mother, Lorraine (Barbara Hershey). Women are thus depicted as exercising much of the agency in the film through their leadership, while masculinity becomes associated with toxic passivity.

While Renai is introduced as the active parent, Josh is first shown as passive. Renai is seen surrounded by the din of the hissing tea kettle, crying baby, and noisy boys in the kitchen, and Josh is immersed in silence upstairs. Alone in the privacy of the upstairs bathroom, he is able to enjoy his own space while going through his morning routine uninterrupted. The film makes a point of highlighting his mundane routine: brushing his teeth, examining his reflection in the mirror, and even plucking a gray hair. He is able to indulge in self-care, knowing that his wife is downstairs taking care of the children and even him. Still on the phone attempting to talk to a human agent, Renai must also tie her husband's tie. Although she has been central to the children, all attention now turns to their father, who is able to laugh and joke with the boys and caress the baby's cheek; later, he brings a bag of dinosaur toys home for his boys. The distinction between the two parents is clear: Josh is the jovial, "fun" parent, while Renai is the responsible one.

This distinction stems from Josh's passivity and avoidance in terms of domestic duties. When Renai asks if he is going to take their sons to school or pick them up, he answers: "I can't . . . I can't. I have a PTA meeting. I totally forgot." His responses read as excuses, curtailing his parental role in favor of his professional one and choosing to not be active in his role as a parent to his own children. Instead, he chooses to be active in his role as a teacher, a position that connotes parenting of students. She is deprived of even voicing her reaction, however, as he kisses her and leaves before she can respond, casting him as dismissive of the domestic realities of the family. Kali cries, an action that causes an immediate response from Renai while Josh walks out of the room with an indifferent goodbye of "I'll see you guys." He enters to a scene of chaos only to depart from one, all while not taking any action to alleviate the distress.

The active-versus-passive dichotomy of parenthood continues with how each parent reacts to Dalton's mysterious coma. Josh remains largely removed from the situation at home and is instead shown as away from the house, sleeping in his classroom late at night. Similar to the earlier scene in the bathroom, he enjoys the privacy of this quiet space. Yet just as his reflection in the mirror during that initial scene would later act as a portal to his possession in the Further, so too does his aloneness in the classroom make him vulnerable. Although physically distanced from the home, the chalkboard behind Josh's head reveals a drawing of the demon attempting to possess Dalton.

Whereas Josh is able to inhabit spaces of his own, Renai is largely tethered to the physical home. When she approaches the subject with him, he uses his position as financial provider against her in saying: "What choice do I have? Gotta pay Dalton's bills." His answer shows his detachment from his family and the domestic situation, phrasing it in a way that implies that his son is a financial burden. Renai is the parent who takes on the primary caretaker responsibilities of Dalton while he remains hooked up to machines, including changing his sheets and tubes. Renai, likewise, is the parent who observes the supernatural occurrences the most. A commonality among many of these supernatural incidents is the role of the baby monitor and the baby crying; the two often herald the appearance of a supernatural entity. When Renai checks on her daughter, she sees a pale figure in the room. The security alarm sounds through the house as Renai witnesses the spirits invade her home, while Josh remains downstairs investigating the cause of the mysterious noises.

Josh continues his refusal to accept the circumstances, lashing out at Renai and rejecting Elise's help. He exclaims, "I can't have someone coming into our home and telling us the reason our son is in a coma is because his soul has floated off to another dimension. . . . I did this to make you feel at ease, and if it helped, great." He follows this up, saying that "to bring Dalton into it" is going too far. His comment points to the division of the problem in his mind: Renai's anxiety and Dalton's coma. To Josh, the two problems are separate. Not acknowledging the connection between Renai's anxiety and Dalton's coma shows Josh's compartmentalization of domestic issues.

He blames Renai rather than working to solve the issues at hand, remarking, "Don't you see, Renai? You want to believe anybody." And he reminds her, "I moved houses for you," continuing: "What do you mean I don't believe you? I'm on your side here. But this is dangerous and exploitative." He tells Elise and her assistants: "You guys come into the home of a seriously ill child and to make some tenuous connection between him and the images my wife is seeing. Voila. Tears validate the power. Here's your six hundred dollars." His reference to money harkens back to his earlier comment to Renai about his need to pay for Dalton's bills. His words emphasize his reliance on physical tangibility as safety: houses, money, and physical bodies are, to him, proof of normalcy.

To save their son, Josh must become an active parent. Elise and Lorraine explain that Lorraine knew to call her because years ago Josh suffered from a spirit attempting to possess him; that it is from Josh that Dalton has his ability to astral project. Lorraine explains:

> When you were about eight, you suffered night terrors and these awful fits and pure fear. You were terrified of an old woman who used to come visit you at night. I told you to grow up, and then I saw her for myself. [Pulls out old photographs that show Josh with a blurred woman in the background.] At first, I thought it was a camera problem. And then I saw her again. In each photo, she got closer and closer and closer to you.

Now, to save his son, Josh must remember what he can no longer remember. The reveal also showcases the root cause of the family's problems: it was not the individual houses that were haunted but the father. In returning to the Further and resurrecting the repressed, Josh is challenged to directly confront his masculinity and parenthood.

Only when Josh asks for a sign from Dalton that his son is still present in the physical world does Josh receive his answer. Josh stares at Dalton's drawings on the wall and sees that the subjects and text under the images reveal that Elise was, in fact, correct in her analysis of the supernatural. It takes a physical gesture to allow Josh to accept Elise's help, even after both his wife and mother echo their concerns. For it to come from his young son and not any of the adult women in his life elevates his character into one with misogynistic undertones. His dismissive attitude and passivity, thus, can be reinterpreted as condescending and controlling as he tries to maintain order in his destabilized family.

The film highlights the supportive strength of mother-to-mother relationships as Renai finds comfort in Josh's mother, Lorraine, since they both have experiences with the supernatural. Renai says that her mother-in-law must think her crazy.[4] Lorraine, however, shows herself to be the opposite of her son in Renai's time of need, stating, "Nobody, not me or anybody, knows what you're going through right now. . . . Whatever you have to do to get through it, do it. And you don't have to apologize for anything." When Josh chides Renai for bringing in a priest to try to solve the problems, Lorraine defends her:

> What's happening to Renai is real. I've seen it for myself. I came today because last night I had a dream about this place. I was in this house, but it was late at night. I was afraid. I went into your bedroom, but you were both asleep. I knew I was asleep in the dream, but I could feel that someone was awake and in the house. I went into Dalton's room. There was something in there with him. It was standing there in the corner. I asked it, "Who are you?" And it said it was a visitor. I said, "What do you want?" It said, "Dalton." I can still hear that voice.

Elise deduces that Dalton is not in a coma; instead, he has astral projected his spiritual body too far into another realm, which she calls the Further, "a world beyond our own yet it's all around us. A place without time as we know it . . . a dark realm filled with the tortured souls of the dead. A place not meant for the living." She explains that that the spirits Renai sees are trying to access his physical body, and there is a demon as well, "who seeks Dalton's body for one reason: to cause pain to others." Through her role and history with the Lamberts, Elise becomes a surrogate mother to the characters. She is purposely dressed in modern clothing to have her outward presence be more mundane than supernatural, becoming another female character who acts as a mother to sons. In her case, her two assistants, Specs and Tucker, take on surrogate son roles in their relationship.

She likewise plays the role of exorcist in the film in guiding Josh through the Further and expelling the demon from Dalton's body. Although Elise is costumed in ordinary clothing, her assistants, Specs and Tucker, are typically dressed like missionaries, with matching white dress shirts and ties. As Dalton's body becomes possessed and controlled by the demon during a séance, Elise grabs Dalton by the head and shouts, "Leave this vessel!" In doing so, the film subverts the traditional exorcism scene in which a male exorcist expels a possessing entity from a female body. Armando Maggi explains:

> Despite their efforts, these fictional exorcists often fail in their endeavor or their success is marred by negative consequences. The core of the represen-

tation is habitually the female body in pain strapped to a chair or a bed. Structured like thrillers, horror films on possessions often depict an unexpected reversal in which a central character who seemed harmless and virtuous becomes the embodiment of radical evil. In most cases, this sudden revelation concerns the possessed person herself. (780)

The possessed body in *Insidious* furthers this subversion through its departure from an emblem of evil. Instead, the film makes Dalton's coma central to his possession, thereby preserving his child body and innocence. Elise reprises her role of exorcist in *Insidious: Chapter 2* when she destroys Michelle's spirit in the Further to free its hold on Josh's body. Even then, the sequel film follows suit in clearly reprieving Josh of responsibility while his body is possessed by making it clear that his soul is located elsewhere. In showing the father as the savior, the movie harkens back to *The Exorcist*, in which it must be the father that saves the son, not the mother, to establish harmony in the family, falling within the realm of traditional gender roles.

Elise instructs Josh to "keep a steady stride," a phrase intended to inspire bravery and masculinity as he enters the Further. Once in the astral plane, Josh first encounters his eight-year-old self who points him in the right direction to begin his journey; he must first start in their old home, where the supernatural experiences first happened. In this house, he sees a woman in a white wedding dress ascend the stairs, an image that connects to the earlier photograph of Renai from her wedding day. He hears crying and goes into a nearby empty room to see a woman in the corner, paralleling Renai's own feelings of trapped frustration and sadness. He hears a laughing child in the hallway, a singular sound he evoked amongst his own children. Downstairs, he hears music and sees a woman at an ironing board in a dress; the husband sits on the couch with a newspaper, and the daughter sits next to him. The only movement from the scene is when the woman blinks. Josh then goes into the parlor to see the daughter with a shotgun; gunshots are heard while the family is shown dead. The family is then resurrected and smiles at Josh. The image of this happy-turned-tragic family is representative of Josh's static perception of his family in their home. Although the outcome is not murderous, his stasis caused destructive forces to escalate to the point of his son's life being in danger.

As he ascends into the attic, he sees the red door that was in Dalton's drawing. Keeping guard at this door is a male spirit who stalked and licked

Renai in their first home, an action that exerts sexual and masculine dominance. The spirit attacks Josh, trying to choke him. Elise coaches him from
the outside, saying: "You're stronger than they are, Josh. You are the one
who is alive." Her reminder coaxes him to defeat the entity; in doing so, he
asserts his own dominance. On the other side of the door, Josh sees lit red
candles and hears Dalton crying. Josh goes to his son, reassuring him that
"Daddy's here." Whereas the film started with Dalton wearing pajamas that
matched Renai's, he now wears ones that match Josh's shirt, showing that
it is now his father that surrounds and protects him, affirming Josh's connection to his son.

He hears music from a theater box above him, and the camera shows the
red-and-black-faced demon has puppets, presumably representative of his
victims over the years given his earlier puppetry of Dalton's physical body.
The demon's appearance is very childlike, similar to how a child would imag-
ine the devil: the color red, eerie music, and puppetry associate the entity
with a childlike appearance. When the demon emerges, viewers see that the
entity has hooves as feet, again associating it with an iconic image of a devil.
Dalton's surroundings can also be seen as a childlike projection of hell, with
him chained inside of a smoke-filled pit with archaic, demonic statues surrounding him. The space questions the appearance of entities and the layout
of the Further, suggesting that objects appear as the individual characters
perceive them rather than how they actually are.

Although Josh is able to free his son and the pair appear to make it safely
back into the land of the living, the film does not end on a happy note.
Instead, Josh is confronted by the spirit from his childhood: the woman in
the black wedding dress. He becomes distracted by her presence when leaving
the Further, shouting: "I'm not scared of you! Get away from me! Get away
from me! Leave me alone!" His ability to become distracted and his taunts to
her regress him from an adult man saving his child to a child himself; rather
than destroying his own demon, he tries to push it away. Because of this, it
is later implied that it was not the real Josh who returned from the Further;
instead, a camera flash and picture reveal that the spirit traded places with
Josh in the Further. Elise discovers this secret; however, before she can warn
the family, the possessed Josh chokes her. Renai sees the last picture that Elise
took of Josh and the spirit. The final words of the film come from Josh who
says, "Renai, I'm right here," ending the movie on a cliffhanger and setting
up for the plot of the sequel, *Insidious: Chapter 2*.

Memory

Insidious: Chapter 2 quickly picks up from the ending of the first movie. Renai and Josh are staying with Lorraine because their rental home is under investigation following the death of Elise. Despite her death, Elise is not mourned or grieved by the family she helped save as the characters struggle with the issue of memory. Renai is convinced that there are still supernatural entities in the home, Dalton is recovered from his experiences, though still able to astral project, and Josh is eager to move on with their lives to regain a sense of normalcy in the family. Memory becomes associated with disruption and destabilization; the repression of memory, therefore, becomes a coping mechanism for trauma. Unlike its predecessor, *Insidious: Chapter 2* forces characters to revisit sites of memory to process fragmented trauma in order to recompose the shattered, destabilized self.

The issue of suppressing trauma and horror is introduced from the beginning. The film opens with a flashback to when Lorraine first contacted Elise about Josh in 1986. Elise interviews a young Josh on camera, asking him about his dreams. He says: "I see myself sleeping . . . somewhere dark. It's always dark here. She's here. She says she's a friend. She visits me every night." At the time, Lorraine was a single mother working full time at the hospital. The spirit can then be seen as acting on the family's instability by offering to fill the void left by his mother's forced absence. Lorraine explains to Elise, "My day job makes raising my son a night job." Josh's description of the woman haunting his dreams is fitting since his words reveal her constant presence in his life, filling the void left by his mother's absence. The absence of a parent connects with the first movie, showing that the supernatural and subsequent trauma from the hauntings are inherited.

After conducting an investigation, Elise concludes that this spirit is a "parasite" rather than a friend. She offers to take away Josh's ability to travel into the Further, and Lorraine instructs Elise to "make him forget." This solution does not address the problem itself; instead, it allows for Lorraine to control the narrative of her son's childhood. Later, when Lorraine reaches out to Specs and Tucker to help her with the unusual disturbances in her home, she admits, when Elise first came to help her in 1986, "I did a lot to try to forget that part of my life." Her words hint at her desire to forget the supernatural and the guilt in not being able to be as physically present in her son's life. Lorraine later confronts this in revisiting the now-abandoned hospital where she used

to work to uncover answers behind the identity of the woman in black: Parker
Crane (Tom Fitzpatrick), a former patient of hers. This reveal affirms the connections between her guilt and the supernatural, with a flashback showing
that Parker chose Lorraine's son while he was still alive, when Josh came to
the hospital one day to see his mother as she was working.

DESIRE FOR NORMALCY

Josh's problematic treatment of women continues in this film in his relationship with his mother. Lorraine investigates the house and sees a figure
walking around the home. Josh tells her, "There is no one here because if
there was that would scare my family, and I don't need Renai hearing any of
that stuff right now." In a change from the original film, he insists on taking
his sons to school. Although this may seem like a well-meaning gesture and
posit him as an active parent, it is actually so that she can relax and rest; as
such, his action is a refusal to address the deeper underlying issue.

Even when Renai is physically attacked, Josh continues to be adamant
about his insistence on normalcy, much like Guy from *Rosemary's Baby* and
George from *The Amityville Horror*. Josh, consequently, is another character
in the line of dismissive men toward women's fear and pain. She insists that
they move again, a suggestion that would repeat the action of the first film.
Josh reminds her of this fact and explains: "You have to just not be afraid. You
have to relax." This response casts Renai in the role of a hysterical woman,
invalidating her emotions so as to control her. She pushes back against him,
saying that she cannot relax and feels as if they are already dead. Josh rebuffs
this, arguing: "They have no power over you. All you have to do is ignore
them, and they will go away." His reassurance that ignoring the ever-present
spirits will make them disappear is childlike: like pictures in a book, all one
has to do is simply look the other way, and they are no longer there.

While alone in the house, one of the baby's toys moves on its own from
the room where it was. Renai goes to see who could have caused it and sees
Michelle singing, "Row, row, row your boat . . ." as her voice is then heard on the
baby monitor ending the rhyme "life is but a dream." Renai hears her daughter
cry, but when she attempts to see her, the door to the baby's room closes in
front of her as she hears a woman scream, "Don't you dare!" Once inside, the
spirit quickly slaps Renai across the face, rendering her unconscious. The

spirit prevents Renai from enacting her maternal agency in checking on Kali; in doing so, it forces Renai to become physically immobilized and inactive.

When Josh returns, he finds Renai on the floor in this condition. He lifts her up and puts her on the couch. He sniffs her, an action that is animalistic and predatory. He removes a tooth from the back of his mouth, showing the distance between the spirit and the physical body. The possessing spirit whispers to him, "Your dead soul is killing its living skin," and it instructs him to kill Renai or else he will "waste away." His possession pushes him to a place of hypermasculinity, urging him to kill his wife in order to feel strong and powerful. The pulling of the tooth possibly refers to Freud's interpretation of dreams in which the pulled tooth signifies the pulling of the penis in an act of masturbation. Creed points out, however, when a tooth is pulled out by someone else, it can represent castration instead (117). The organization of this scene points to that of castration. The scene takes place after Lorraine reveals that Parker was admitted to the hospital because he did, in fact, try to castrate himself. Since Parker is possessed by his mother, the pulling of the tooth can be read through the lens of castration, stressing her point that without killing Renai, his masculinity will continue to be challenged.

The realization that the Josh that viewers come to understand is actually possessed by the murderous spirit of Parker Crane appears toward the end of the film. The possessed Josh announces to the real-life spirit of Josh: "You're trying to reach her, but you won't. Not from over there. Shadows are your home now." Josh's spirit attempts to contact Renai by moving Kali's musical toy around on its own and playing the song she wrote for him on the piano. As Renai explains to Lorraine, "Last time when I looked into his eyes . . . I didn't recognize him." Lorraine explains to Renai: "It's not the house. It's Josh." She continues: "I think when Josh went into that other world, something else came back. We believe it's a spirit that's killed many times before and will kill again." As in the first film, Kali proves pivotal as it is her boisterous toy that alerts Renai to the presence of a spirit.

Renai Evolved

Just as in the first film, Renai is the one who first notices the hauntings. She hears music playing downstairs and hears a baby crying, even though Kali is asleep. She sees Kali on the floor instead of inside of her crib, where she placed her. Renai explains all of this to Josh, who tries to explain the incidents as mundane happenings. Unlike in the first film, Renai is more direct with her husband. In regard to his nonchalant attitude, she asks him, "What is wrong with you?" In pushing back against her husband, Renai demonstrates an evolved self that is more independent from Josh. The following conversation takes place:

> JOSH: I just want us to move on from this. That's all. I want us to be a normal family.
> RENAI: There is nothing normal about this. These things are still here. Elise is dead; no one is talking about it. Someone murdered her!
> JOSH: Then let's talk about it. You think I did it?
> RENAI: No.
> JOSH: Good. Because I know what happened. I went into that place to get our son back and something evil followed me and killed Elise. You saw it. You saw those things. Listen to me, nothing is going to bother us. Not anymore. We have our family back. We have our son. Isn't that what we should be focusing on?

Josh's insistence on normalcy involves suppressing the trauma and horror he went through during his childhood and in *Insidious*. Although Josh initially opens up the conversation to talk about Elise's murder, he only seeks reassurance that Renai does not think he killed her. Once he hears that, he pivots the conversation back to recounting his time in the Further and insisting that they are no longer impacted by the events of the first film. He reminds Renai of his role in saving their son, asserting his role as protector and patriarch. To him, this newfound focus on family includes forgetting the past, just as his mother did when he was younger.

Renai's instincts prove to be correct on several accounts. Not only is the family still haunted by the events of their previous homes, but there is something wrong with her husband: he is, in fact, possessed. The spirit occupying Josh's physical body is not his own; instead, it is that of Parker Crane. Parker Crane's spirit is one in flux and never truly his own, even while alive. During his life, he was traumatized by his mother Michelle who insisted that Parker forget that he was a boy. She abused and coerced him into a female identity, Marilyn. She forced him to wear very feminine clothing, a blonde wig, and would abuse him if he deviated from this identity. Later in his adult life, Parker was hospitalized for trying to castrate himself and died by suicide.

Her name for Parker, Marilyn, is similar to her own, Michelle. This similarity extends beyond the name as she was also the one who birthed Parker's murderous habits, dressing up in a black wedding dress and veil and murdering young women. The ghost of a young Parker tells the psychic Carl (Steven Coulter) in the Further, "If she [his mother] sees you, she'll make me kill you." Her child was used as a projection of her own monstrous identity. She abused Parker so that they transformed into the Bride in Black, while she, herself, could remain the Woman in White. This aligns with the Bride in Black's method of torturing and killing victims, tying them up in a cocoon-like fabric wrapping as Parker applies the necessary makeup to become the physical embodiment of his murderous self. The victims' bodies are found behind a wall in the Crane home. They are lined up in wooden pews with cloth covering them. The image can be both that of a womb and that of a veil covering a bride's face before the wedding.

TRAUMA EXPLORED

The history of Parker Crane is explored in the Further. Carl and Elise's spirit see a portrait of Parker's mother and a young girl in pigtails. The portrait reads "Mater Mortis" or "Mother of Death." Behind a bookcase, they find bodies with molded sheets over them and surgical equipment on a shelf. Newspaper clippings reveal headlines that read "Bride in Black, the Serial Killer" and "Old Woman Dressed in a Black Wedding Gown and Veil," who claimed more than a dozen victims. It is revealed that Parker Crane is the so-called Bride in Black serial killer, who killed for his mother because she forced him to. He targeted Josh as a victim because he wanted to reclaim the masculine childhood that was stolen from him. The Bride in Black and the Woman in White are opposites in terms of the color of their costuming. Together, they present two halves—black and white—that come together to possess Josh.

The entwined identities of Parker and his mother merge into one: the possessing, murderous spirit that inhabits Josh's body. As Parker explains to Renai:

She wanted me to kill you, but I said no. But now I know she was right. . . . You are a miserable, ungrateful bitch. You have no idea how you have wasted your life being afraid of the dead because pretty soon you are going to be one of them. When I take you in my home in the dark, you'll realize how happy you should have been for your brief little moment in the sun.

The Bride in Black's victims seated in pews. © Sony Pictures.

He says this while on top of her and pointing a finger at her; body language that is sexual and violent. He attempts to choke her to death but is interrupted by Dalton, who hits him with a baseball bat. The action matures Dalton as a masculine protector of Renai—a significance that is continued when it is Dalton who uses his ability to reenter the Further to find Josh. He is no longer the little boy who needs to be saved; instead, he is the one who becomes the savior.

To free Josh from the possessing entities, Elise's spirit and the real spirit of Josh must destroy Michelle's spirit in the Further to remove her hold on Josh's body. They go back to Parker's childhood home where a confrontation between young Parker (Tyler Griffin) and his mother takes place. He shouts, "My name is Parker!" His mother holds a picture he drew for her with yellow flowers and butterflies on it that is addressed "To Mommy, love Parker." His picture is not only meant as a gesture of love but also shows the deeper desire to placate his mother through choosing the gender-neutral yellow. Rather than accepting this token of affection, his mother rejects it and her son in the process. She interrogates him, asking: "What is this? Did you do this?" When Parker denies it, she shrieks, "Don't you dare!" And she slaps him hard across his face, telling him, "Speak the truth." When he admits that he drew it, she crumples it up and shouts: "Parker is not your name! That is the name your father gave you. Your name is Marilyn. Do you understand? Repeat after me. My name is Marilyn. Say it!" An abused Parker repeats the name his mother forces on him and is rewarded with a soothed tone from her as she says: "Quiet now. You'll be a good little girl." Although his mother's

Michelle (Danielle Bisutti), also known as Mater Mortis, reminds her child (Tyler Griffin) that they are Marilyn, not Parker. © Sony Pictures.

motivations are never explicit, the context surrounding her character provides insight into her role as a single mother raising her child. Her desire for her son to reject his identity shows a forced queering of his body. Her association between quietness and goodness conform to traditional notions of femininity. The contrast between her own quiet tone and shrill screams hint at her own struggles with identity. Parker himself affirms his masculinity in shouting his real name. Her use of violence and shouting, both deviations from traditional feminine gender norms, can be read as utilized in order to maintain her maternal authority over her perceived unruly child.

Michelle repeats this association of goodness with young girls while strangling Josh in the spirit world, telling him, "Little girls need to learn to be good." On the surface, her words appear out of place in her attack on Josh. Yet they can again show her feelings toward women and girls, linking submissiveness with femininity. Elise kills Michelle with a rocking horse, a traditional symbol of boyhood and emerging masculinity that is carefully placed throughout the first and second films: next to young Josh's bed, in Foster's bedroom, as well as along the wall of Parker's childhood room. There is even a horse statue in the demon's home in *Insidious*.

The contrast between Elise and Michelle is significant. Elise, even in death, acts as the good, nurturing mother. Once Michelle dies, the possessing spirits leave Josh's body, allowing his spirit to reenter. Elise's actions are the resolution to the problem underlying both films. Her maternal agency restores balance to the family. Rather than remain in the afterlife, she is shown as choosing to return in spirit to assist Specs and Tucker with cases. A positive maternal figure in life, she remains that way in death.

REPRESSION CONTINUED

The movie ends with Josh and Dalton repressing their ability to astral project. Josh tells Carl: "We're ready to forget, once and for all. No more travel. This is the only world we want to be in." While this might seem like a happy ending, it only serves to perpetuate the larger issue of forgetting in the series. Rather than being able to actually process their individual traumas and move forward with their lives in the process, the choice to forget only builds the foundation for another astral house to store repressed memories and trauma. The Further will always remain overlapped with the land of the living, its inhabitants forever present. Just like the haunting lullaby at the end of *Rosemary's Baby*, pain and identity have seemingly been erased in favor of restricted roles.

CHAPTER 5

Mother as Exorcist
The Conjuring and *The Conjuring 2*

The previous two chapters explored the intertwining of the house with the supernatural and the impact on the nuclear families that live there, particularly mothers. Although *The Conjuring* and *The Conjuring 2* follow a similar pattern, the films build on the *Insidious* films, raising the stakes for the possessed individual and family in question through threatening the destruction of the mother (*The Conjuring*) and child (*The Conjuring 2*). In doing so, it brings into question the power of exorcism by positing the power to complete the rite within the maternal. The first film is inspired by the real-life haunting of the Perron family, otherwise known as the Harrisville haunting in which the Perron family—the father, Roger (Ron Livingston), the mother Carolyn, and their five daughters—move into a house inhabited by multiple spirits, the most problematic of which is the spirit of a witch who possesses mothers to kill their own children. Although the family first tries to dismiss the supernatural occurrences, when the incidents escalate, they reach out to Ed and Lorraine Warren, renowned paranormal investigators. The second film follows a similar plot by being based on another real-life haunting, known as the Enfield haunting, for which the Warrens were called upon. The second film, however, raises the stakes from the first through shifting from a nuclear family to a single-parent family and by the victim of possession being a child, not an adult.

Set in 1971 and 1977, *The Conjuring* and *The Conjuring 2* connect with the two previously discussed horror films that were released in the 1970s:

The Exorcist and *The Amityville Horror*. In a review for *Variety* magazine, Justin Chang acknowledges this connection, saying, "While it owes an obvious debt to the likes of 'The Exorcist,' 'Poltergeist' and 'The Amityville Horror' (itself inspired by the Warrens' most famous case), this exuberantly creepy supernatural shocker . . . taps into the sly, self-aware vein of humor that has long been one of Wan's trademarks."[1] The "obvious debt" Chang references emerges in both films through the use of the haunted-house trope in which a family resides in a house with an implied supernatural presence and through the spectacle of the possessed female body seen throughout the films. The first *Conjuring* very much takes a page from *The Amityville Horror* in that a family buys a home to make a new start only to find out that the house they bought is, in fact, haunted; both films also showcase the move as a socioeconomic move as well as a physical one. While there are class differences between Chris MacNeil in *The Exorcist* and Peggy Hodgson (Frances O'Connor) in *The Conjuring 2*, the pair share the commonality of being struggling single mothers with possessed adolescent daughters.

The Conjuring and *The Conjuring 2* are films considered to be part of the recent trope in horror known as the housing-crisis trope, a departure from found-footage-style horror films that emphasize a return to classical aesthetic elements situated within the domestic, such as "antique sofas, ornate antiques, detailed woodwork" along with "chiaroscuro lighting, and vintage décor" (Wessels 512). Emanuelle Wessels draws from the work of Sarah Ahmed in saying that this trope has produced an affective economy of dread and anxiety:

> *Affective economies* refer to the structures that enable affects, or pre-symbolic feelings such as fear, dread, and revulsion, to manifest as products of circulation among bodies and signifiers. In the signifying economy of post-realist horror film, affects of dread and anxiety, coupled, manifest through constitutive relationships among bodies, recording technologies, and antique objects. Fear, within this system, is produced through the realization of the approach of an identifiable object, akin, in horror film, to the visual assault of a monstrous image. Anxiety, conversely, is a "mode of attachment to objects," continually traveling from one to the other in search of something to definitively "stick" to. (512, emphasis original)

In Wessels's paradigm of affective economies, the "identifiable object" that produces fear in both films is the house itself. Within the house, the affect of anxiety is caused by the otherworldly inhabitants of the domestic space, whose territory is disrupted by the arrival of the Perron family in the first film and the Ouija board in the second. More specifically, the ghost Bathsheba (Joseph Bishara) produces the most anxiety since she is the one who attaches onto the family, attempting to break them apart through her possession of Carolyn. In *The Conjuring 2*, the ghost of Bill Wilkins and the demon Valak produce anxiety through Bill's attachment to his old armchair and Valak's possession of Janet.

In each film, the Warrens are depicted as embodiments of Christian goodness sent to rid demonic entities from homes to restore peace. The costuming often points to the characters' roles in exorcising the homes. Ed can be seen wearing black vests and shirts, rendering him a symbolic priest. In contrast, Lorraine is shown wearing white outfits, whose details, such as ruffled collars and lacy sweaters, depict her as a more angelic force. It is ultimately Lorraine who is able to expel the demonic despite Ed's recitation of the exorcism ritual. In doing so, the movies break away from earlier possession films in which it is was the return of the father that led to salvation; instead, it is the mothers' contributions that ultimately lead to resolution for the family in peril.

HOUSING THE SUPERNATURAL

The family in peril in the first movie is a nuclear one leaving an urban environment in favor of a rural Rhode Island farmhouse. It is, in fact, the house that first sees the Perron family and not the other way around. The camera angle purposefully shows the house's perspective: first, in the middle of the parlor and then moving closer to the pale-pink-laced window to see the new occupants. Throughout the chaos of the family moving into the house, the camera continues to be placed in a way that appears to be from inside of the house as if the house itself is hearing the outside characters and watching them come and go from the doorway. The lyrics "What's your name? / Who's your daddy?" play as the family moves in to add to this sense that the house is watching and asking these questions of its new inhabitants.[2] The emphasis is on the family moving inside of the house and on claiming space through furniture, from directing the movers where to place objects to the girls clamoring for room selection. There is more life inside the house, so the house as a character begins to take on life as an observer. Later, when Ed, Lorraine, and their assistant, Drew (Shannon Kook), set up the cameras and equipment to document any supernatural phenomena, the camera moves quickly around from the hallway's perspective. The song "In the Room Where You Sleep" plays. The beginning lyrics are emphasized: "I saw something / Sitting on your bed / I saw something / Touching your head / In the room / Where you sleep."[3] The use of songs in conjunction with the camera and action show the house as an organic being trying to communicate with the characters.

It is clear that the house cost Roger and Carolyn much financially. They bought it at auction from the bank, unaware of the history of its previous occupants. The implication is that they bought it as a foreclosure for presumably less money than a regular house. Roger is a blue-collar worker in his role as a truck driver. In one scene, he is on the phone with a supervisor, trying to negotiate a trip; although the trip would only be half of his normal rate, he agrees to take it for the money. He tells Ed: "I don't know where we'd move to. We got all the money tied up in this place. . . . I don't know who's going to take in a family of seven indefinitely." Whereas Ed is often shown in sweater vests and academic settings, Roger is often shown wearing denim and in the home. When he returns, he finds the house in chaos: eldest daughter Andrea (Shanley Caswell) is being attacked by an invisible force upstairs, the girls are screaming, and Carolyn is trapped in the basement. The message is clear: when father is away, the spirits will play and upset the family structure.

Carolyn sees the potential of the house. She tells Roger, "It's going to be great," talking about the house in the future tense. Roger, however, thinks it's great already. The first time they see the basement, filled with a mix of covered objects, such as furniture, a piano, and more remnants from the previous owners, Carolyn looks around at everything and comments, "This is going to take some serious elbow grease." She believes that it's "just a lot of junk the previous owner didn't want." Roger speculates that "there might be some antiques" in the basement "worth a lot of money," and regardless of whether or not it's worth money, it's theirs now. Carolyn makes it clear that she has no interest in going through the past, however, telling Roger to "knock [himself] out" going through all the materials. Instead, she goes upstairs to make coffee, while Roger says he will work on getting the furnace working. This scene reveals contrasting attitudes toward the home. Carolyn, wishing to start fresh in the house, sees the furniture and other remnants from previous owners as discarded material memories that are not their own; as such, they warrant being removed from the home so that the Perrons can claim the domestic space for themselves. In contrast, Roger sees the materialistic value in keeping these objects, seeing them as capitalistic and of material worth that the family can use to build wealth. Both characters view the basement as an opportunity to build their family's legacy in the house but in different ways.

This scene parallels the next in which a reporter (Arnell Powell) enters the Warrens' basement. Unlike the exposed walls of the Perron house, the Warrens' house is lined with richly floral wallpaper; the contrast between the two homes clearly shows the class differences between the two. The Perron basement is filled with furniture, some covered and some exposed, along with a piano, creating an image of an actively used space. The Warren basement is more crowded and cramped with an array of haunted artifacts that appear as typical items found in a basement: old toys, furniture, and various knickknacks. The connection between material objects and the home is highlighted in the dialogue between the interviewer and Ed:

> REPORTER: So, all these are taken from cases you've investigated?
> ED: Everything you see here is either haunted, cursed, or has been used in some kind of ritualistic practice. . . . Nothing's a toy, not even the toy monkey. . . . Don't touch it.
> REPORTER: Doesn't it scare you to have all these items in your home?
> ED: That's why we have a priest that comes by once a month to bless the room. The way I see it, it's safer for these things to be in here than out there—kind of like keeping guns off the streets.
> REPORTER: Why not just throw them in the incinerator?
> ED: That would only destroy the vessel. Sometimes it's better to keep the genie in the bottle.

Ed positions he and Lorraine as the higher authorities when it comes to the occult, acting as law enforcement for the supernatural through his comparison to the objects in the room to guns on the streets. This is seen from the beginning of the film where they share accounts of their investigations to a room filled with mostly college students to warn them about the dangers of the supernatural.[4] His comparison to their work to keeping guns off the streets likewise portrays them as moral authorities, in addition to ones on the occult. The supernatural objects displayed there very much showcase the material memory associated with them, so much so that they can no longer be defined by their original intended use; instead, they are defined by the dark moments they were part of. The scenes act to remind viewers of the fluidity of objects and materialism: they can define spaces, homes, and families.

The lighting of the interior of the Perrons' house is physically darker than the Warrens' to show the different relationships between the supernatural and family life. Not only is the home darker, but it is also dirtier since the previous family moved without cleaning it. This is opposed to the Warrens' own home with its brightly wallpapered hallways and spotless carpets. There is no paint or wallpaper on the walls in the Perron farmhouse; instead, photographs are used to decorate and line the walls and, in the process, help cover up the cracks. While the Warrens' home features many haunted objects, the supernatural is contained in the basement, reflecting the stable family unit.

The only time the supernatural disrupts the Warren family in *The Conjuring* is when Lorraine leaves behind a locket in the Perrons' basement. The locket is part of a matching pair that Lorraine's daughter, Judy (Sterling Jerins), gifted her to wear when she is away from her; inside of Lorraine's locket is a photograph of her daughter. Together these lockets create a material bond between mother and daughter. Using the locket as a conduit, Bathsheba targets Judy by waking her, and she gets out of bed. Judy wanders the wallpapered halls, calling out for her parents and grandmother before descending below. The basement door is ajar, adding suspense to the scene by questioning if something was released. Judy wanders into her father's study, where she sees Bathsheba rocking in the rocking chair with the Annabelle doll, combing her hair. The door to the study locks by itself, and Annabelle turns her head toward Judy. Judy's pleas are answered just in time as her father and mother arrive home and Ed is able to open the door right before the rocking chair flies toward Judy's head.

The choice of attack is significant because the head is often targeted with women in the movie. Bathsheba hung herself, snapping the connection between her head and neck; she likewise convinced Rory's mother to do the same. Andrea is pulled by her hair around the room with onlookers. The rocking chair is hurled toward Judy's head in Ed's study. The head thus serves to redefine women's roles in the movie: it is not the men, but the women who are the dominant forces that drive the families. In unsettling their own home and attacking their daughter, the supernatural incident acts to propel the Warrens' investigation and cleaning of the Perron house.

POSSESSION AND EXORCISM

Bathsheba's possession initially manifests itself by means of Carolyn's physical body, marking the relationship as a tactile one. Carolyn awakes with bruises on her leg, shoulder, arm, and collarbone and at first dismisses them as being her own fault when, in reality, it was the result of the ghost making physical contact with her. This creates physical intimacy with the unaware Carolyn. To complete the possession, Bathsheba hovers over Carolyn while she is sleeping and vomits blood into her mouth when she awakes to scream. The scene has an implicit dual sexual quality to it, with the blood symbolizing menstrual blood, similar to that in *The Exorcist*. The blood also takes on a masculine quality as it inseminates Carolyn. The mouth, as the entry point into her body, furthers this reading as it can be read as representative of the vagina or womb. The result is that Bathsheba makes Carolyn a fertile body for possession, attempting to use her against the children she created so as to pervert Carolyn in a way similar to Bathsheba herself.

Bathsheba's possession initially manifests itself the morning after the family moves in. Carolyn wakes to see a bruise on her leg underneath her kneecap and realizes that the house is quite cold. She barely walks out of her room when her oldest daughter, Andrea, asks, "Do you think we could have bought a house with a toilet that actually works?" She continues her barrage, complaining to her mother that there was a weird smell in her room last night. Carolyn asks if it is still there to which Andrea answers no, and Carolyn's response is "problem solved." The pairing of Carolyn's bruised body with her daughter's sarcastic question reflects Carolyn's mental and emotional state. Like the internal bleeding of a bruise, her daughter's comment signals the emotional bruising of Carolyn's motherhood, with each upset working to break down her physical and mental boundaries. Carolyn bluntly tells her to tell her father about it, deferring to Roger to solve the problems of the physical house, while she maintains the internal structure of the family. Instead of focusing on the underlying issues, Carolyn chooses to push ahead, focusing instead on hanging pictures, aiming to embed the family's own story in the house.

Once inside of Carolyn, the demon intends to stay inside her body and inside the house, physically searing and bruising Carolyn when others attempt to remove her from the house and causing the entire house itself to shake, illustrating the connection between Carolyn, Bathsheba, and the domestic space of the home. It is not just Carolyn herself who needs to be

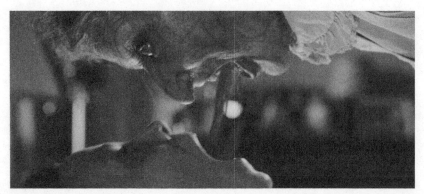

Bathsheba (Joseph Bishara) infects and symbolically impregnates Carolyn (Lili Taylor) to possess her. © Warner Bros. Pictures.

free, but the house itself. This connection is again seen during the exorcism. Ed, Roger, and the Lorraine first attempt to exorcise the demon from Carolyn in the basement and tie her to a chair with rope, implying that the rope they tie her with is the same one Bathsheba and Rory's mother (Carmella Gioio) used to hang themselves with. They throw a sheet over her while Ed reads from the Bible. The placement of the white sheet and rope over Carolyn lends a womb-like imagery to the scene. The setting of this exorcism is seemingly intimate, with an unofficial priest, rope, and cloth the only means separating an aggressively possessed Carolyn from the witnesses. Maggi notes:

> The exorcism of Carolyn Perron is staged as a private and dark representation. A single light bulb, dangling from the ceiling, lights up the area where the young mother is tied to a chair and covered with a sheet. On the one hand, we know that the sheet hides a victim who should not be held responsible for the attempted murder of her child. On the other, the words recited by the lay exorcist trigger such violent reactions in the possessed woman strapped to the chair and such dramatic disarray in the ritual space. . . . Reminiscent of a Christ-like figure, Carolyn looks like a victim subjected to ruthless torture, but her suffering has also something wild and bestial about it. (781–82)

Although Carolyn vomits blood underneath the sheet, the demon still has control over her, and its face emerges from the bloody sheet in a womb-like image of Bathsheba being born from Carolyn's physical body. She breaks free

Bathsheba reborn in Carolyn's possessed body. © Warner Bros. Pictures.

from her restraints and scrambles up the stairs to find the family's youngest daughter, April (Kyla Deaver), to kill her with a pair of scissors, an act that would literally and figuratively sever the ties between mother and child. Her choice of scissors is also important since, in an earlier scene, when Bathsheba grabbed ahold of Andrea and dragged her around the room, Lorraine used the pair of scissors to cut her hair and break her free from the demon's grasp. Carolyn finds her daughter hidden in the walls of the house, the innermost structure of the domestic, and it is the female, maternal power that is able to extinguish the demon.

Lorraine, a fellow mother, places her hand on Carolyn's head and urges her to "fight from the inside," reminding her of the cherished memory of the family at the beach. She screams, "This is your daughter!" as a battle cry for Carolyn to take control and save her family. The placement of the three characters in this scene is worth noting. From the viewer's perspective, Ed is positioned to the right of the possessed Carolyn and commands Bathsheba to reveal herself; his command temporarily allows for Carolyn to detach from Bathsheba and allows Lorraine to speak directly to Carolyn. Lorraine is positioned above Carolyn and Ed, in the middle of the kitchen, a traditionally maternal space. She wears large pearl earrings that the camera zooms in on when highlighting her maternal role in the exorcism, while Ed wears a black vest, symbolizing his connection to the church and to his role as a priestly figure. Taken together, the positioning and costuming of these characters in this scene reenvisions Ed and Lorraine as spiritual entities: the Father (Ed) and the Mother and Holy Spirit (Lorraine).

MATERNAL IDENTITY

Bathsheba's background is very much tied to maternity and the power of the maternal figure; she is a perversion of the nurturing mother. In life, she sacrificed her seven-day-old baby in front of the fireplace and proceeded to climb a tree on the property, declare her love of Satan, curse anyone who would try to take her land, and hung herself. Bathsheba thus becomes emblematic of the abject mother. Kristeva writes, "The other maternal image is tied to suffering, illness, sacrifice, and a downfall. . . . This kind of motherhood . . . is repulsive and fascinating, abject" (158). Carolyn asks Lorraine, "How could a mother kill her own child?" to which she responds: "It was never a child to her. She just used her God-given gift as the ultimate offense against Him. . . . Some believe that it elevates their status in the eyes of Satan." In using the child as a means to elevate her standing, the sacrificial child takes on value as property; considering she curses anyone who tries to take her land, Bathsheba's act of perversion can likewise be read as a woman protecting her property and using the sacrifices of mothers and their children who live there to increase her power and standing.

Her process of possession, infecting mothers so that they kill their own children, substantiates Kristeva's argument that "abjection is elaborated through a failure to recognize its kin; nothing is familiar, not even the shadow of a memory," adding to her role as an abject mother through her function as destroyer rather than creator (5). Her choice of Carolyn gains significance as Carolyn, like Bathsheba, attempts to redefine the land and the house to make it her own, lining the walls with family portraits. The aforementioned dialogue takes place while she hangs family photos, her favorite of which is one with the entire family grouped together on a beach, and Carolyn's comment to Lorraine that that day was a "perfect opportunity for a photo. Start fresh . . . new house, new beginning." This gestures toward the commodification of the house that underlies the scene's nostalgia.

Carolyn appeals to Lorraine's maternal identity in order to have the Warrens investigate their home. She pleads with Lorraine, asking: "Don't you have a daughter? Wouldn't you do anything to protect her? I have five daughters all scared to death." In this way, she is emphasizing the need to protect her family. It is important to note that it is Carolyn, not Roger, who reaches out to the Warrens, enacting the protector role for her family. Bathsheba's choice to possess her, then, is significant due to the nature of possession. As Ed outlines:

[There are] three stages of demonic activity: infestation, oppression, and possession. The infestation . . . that's the whispering, the footsteps, the feeling that there's another presence, which ultimately grows into oppression, the second stage. This is where the victim, and it's usually the one most psychologically vulnerable, is targeted specifically by an external force. Breaks the victim down, crushes their will, and once in a weakened state, leads them to the third and final stage: possession.

Carolyn's psychological vulnerability can be seen as stemming from her dual nurturing maternal and protective paternal roles. Indeed, when Carolyn gets locked in the basement, the voice she calls for is Andrea, her oldest daughter; as the oldest, Andrea is looked at as having the most responsibility and as the surrogate parental figure in her father's absence.

Ed states: "Lorraine and I both feel that what your house needs is a cleansing. An exorcism." He clarifies that an exorcism is not just for people; it also applies to physical objects and structures, such as houses. The term "cleansing" has a dual meaning here: it refers to the spiritual purification that needs to take place and an actual, physical cleansing of the house given its abandoned state for years. Ed and Lorraine aim to cleanse the house in that respect, creating a familial atmosphere that Carolyn and Roger were unable to achieve. Ed cooks pancakes for the family, Lorraine does laundry, and Ed even fixes up an old car Roger was unable to. Carolyn remarks: "House hasn't felt this way in a long time. I think the kids feel a lot safer with you around." In admitting this, Carolyn devalues Roger's role in the relationship. It is clear that Ed is seen as the male protector, not Roger.

While Lorraine helps restore the family order, her help comes at a personal cost. Ed explains: "Whatever Lorraine sees, feels, touches, it helps people, but it also takes a toll on her—a little piece each time." Her psychic abilities transform her into a self-sacrificing mother. Lorraine goes into the structure of the house to better understand what is going on, essentially acting to possess the house in the process through her physical contact. Once inside the structure of the walls, she sees toys hidden in there from Rory, the little boy murdered in the house. When she plays his music box, she sees the noose Rory's mother used to hang herself with after killing him in a possessed state. Lorraine then falls through the rafters into the basement and uses a flashlight to look around, seeing the benches, chairs, and other objects before seeing the ghost of Rory's mother crying over her dead son. Rory's mother

The power of Lorraine's (Vera Farmiga) maternal healing expels Bathsheba and saves Carolyn.
© Warner Bros. Pictures.

says, "She made me do it," as mascara runs down her face. Lorraine hears creaking from the rafters and sees Bathsheba's dangling feet in front of her. As the corpse turns around to face her, Lorraine sees the face of Bathsheba. Rather than confront the spirit, Lorraine runs away from the horror before her. Her experiences take away her control, and consequently, she becomes trapped within the walls of the house and the basement. Lorraine's appeal to Carolyn's motherhood empowers Carolyn to draw on her maternal agency to expel Bathsheba, whereas Ed's exorcism uses more physical tactics in an attempt to expel the demon. Carolyn vomits blood, physically and symbolically rejecting Bathsheba, a white light glows, and the final scene features a now-free Carolyn walking out of the house into the sunshine and the arms of her family. Both instances of light—the white light from the inside and the sunshine outside—hint at the spiritual cleansing of the domestic through Carolyn's reclaiming of the space and her family.

STAGING THE SUPERNATURAL

Whereas the Perron family is a nuclear family under attack by supernatural forces, the Hodgson family is a broken home. Like the first film, *The*

Conjuring 2 is also inspired by a real-life haunting, known as the Enfield haunting. The film portrays the case as one in which the youngest daughter, Janet Hodgson, suddenly becomes seemingly possessed by the spirit of the former homeowner, Bill Wilkins.[5] The home under attack in the sequel is an urban one, as opposed to the rural setting in the first film. Although the investigation of each case is documented, the Perron family in *The Conjuring* were able to retain their privacy in the wake of the supernatural occurrences; however, much like the urban sprawl the Hodgson home is part of, the case in *The Conjuring 2* becomes exposed and open to public attention. The film makes it very clear from the beginning that, this time, the family is already vulnerable even before any supernatural occurrences take place. The song "London Calling" by the Clash plays as the camera introduces viewers to members of the Hodgson family and their socio-economic situation.[6] Peggy is a single mother with four young children to look after in the wake of her husband's affair and fathering twin children with a neighbor. The film makes it clear early on that Peggy has several financial troubles and implies they are connected to her being a single mother cut off from her husband's support. An early scene shows the four children—Margaret, Janet, Johnny, and Billy (Lauren Esposito, Madison Wolfe, Patrick McAuley, Benjamin Haigh)—coming home from school to find their mother on the phone with an agency, seeking child-support payments from her ex-husband. She says: "I am being calm. What I don't understand is why you can't help me. No, he hasn't paid a penny of child maintenance for three months." This scene is important because it is the first scene with the family together. Taking place in the kitchen, the audience sees a tired, frustrated mother on the phone with a bureaucratic agency while her children rummage around the kitchen looking for an afterschool snack. She addresses Janet, who was caught holding a lit cigarette at school, saying, "Janet, are things not bad enough around here that I've got to get a call from your headmistress that says you were caught smoking!" Janet denies the claims, but her mother does not believe her. Peggy smokes a cigarette while she berates her daughter of this alleged misbehavior. Her words appear contradictory but show genuine concern for her daughter's well-being; Peggy does not want Janet to turn out the same way she did. Meanwhile, the other children are looking for food. One opens a scarcely supplied pantry door, and another opens a fridge that is empty aside from a couple of jars. As tension starts to escalate in the kitchen between the

Peggy (Frances O'Conner) struggles to maintain control over her homelife. © Warner Bros. Pictures.

accusations of Janet smoking and lying about it and Janet's staunch denial of guilt, the oldest daughter, Margaret, exits the kitchen, stomping upstairs to make her departure known.

The camera highlights the old armchair in the corner of the living room with a slit in the side as Janet moves upstairs. This armchair plays a significant role in the film since it serves as one of the central haunted objects in the house. It is later revealed that the former occupant, Bill Wilkins, died in that armchair, and it is his figure that still haunts it. Its placement in the corner of the living room by the front door is likewise of note since it serves as a vantage point for the living room, hallway, stairs, and kitchen; in other words, it is almost always visible and acts both as a spatial and haunted focal point for the house.

The home is sparsely decorated with lighting and has exposed walls that emit a sense of decay. There are cracks in the walls, and the furniture is old. Posters of celebrities line the walls of the girls' bedroom as opposed to family photographs, suggesting an aspiration and admiration for higher socioeconomic circumstances. The worn-out leather armchair that acts as a source of paranormal activity is intentionally placed in the corner of the living room by the front door, seemingly hidden in the corner. The crevice between the walls behind the chair is dark and from it creeps a mold-like pattern that creates a vaginal shape. This is significant since it is where the former inhabitant of the house died and where Janet is drawn; it is implied that this is where the initial possession takes place. It is symbolically implied that it is a rotten, festering place that takes hold of the inhabitants—in this case, Janet.

Social Class

The lack of food and finances are simultaneously introduced from the beginning of the film. Viewers are offered a glimpse into the sparce stocks of food, and the youngest, Billy, asks his mother why there are no biscuits. She screams, "We have no bloody biscuits because we have no bloody money!" Later, she brings him up a plate of the cookies he sought earlier, and when he asks about the money, she says, "I was going to give up smoking anyway." Her comment allows viewers to sympathize with her plight and identify her as a self-sacrificing mother. She has many factors working against her: she is divorced, poor, and a single mother. Rather than cast her as a failed mother, she is elevated in her persistence despite her circumstances. She falls asleep with the laundry basket next to her near the foot of the bed, implying that her domestic responsibilities are never done. Peggy is aware of her role encompassing both mother and father in light of her husband's absence. She tells a neighbor, "Now it's like I'm having to do both jobs, and I'm rubbish" before putting the laundry in the washing machine, causing the pipe to burst as well as the underlying tension in the family structure.

Peggy's reliance on government and then academic authorities likewise reveals her social class. She is shown as helpless against the threat that plagues her family.[7] Unlike the Perrons in the first movie, Peggy does not have a husband; instead, she relies on the neighbors across the street as a surrogate familial support network, who take the family in after supernatural occurrences take place at the Hodgson residence. In one scene, Janet finds herself thrown from her bed after tying herself to it with a jump rope, a tie to childhood. Her sister falls asleep with headphones on, making it clear that she wishes to mute the family tension that surrounds her. Both girls, however, are woken up by the hauntings around them. Their beds begin to shake violently, and something bites Janet's shoulder. Peggy investigates the commotion and finds the homemade spirit board under the bed that Janet and her friend made from a cereal box, a choice of material that very much ties the spiritual to the homelife. Peggy addresses the girls, angrily asking: "Have you two been playing with this? Taking turns scaring the wits out of each other?" She continues, "No wonder I can't get a good night's sleep! I don't want to hear another word! Now get back to bed, the lot of you!" Peggy associates her lack of sleep with her children's needs, similar to how she associates no money with not being able to supply food in an earlier scene; both cast her as unable to fully provide for and nurture her family given her status as a single mother. She loses her temper with her children, undermining the traditional maternal archetype. The supernatural act that follows highlights this separation from her family with a dresser slamming up against the door, separating Peggy and her daughters from the boys.

The family runs out of the house across the street to a neighbor's house. Peggy says to her neighbors: "Seen it with my own eyes. Bloody thing went straight across the room." The neighbor believes that it must be someone playing a prank and reassures her that there must be "some sort of explanation" and calls the police. The police hear booming and pounding in the walls of the house. One of the officers pulls a chair from the kitchen, steps on it, and listens to the noise. After they stand on the floor, the chair moves on its own accord and is pushed back into the table. This blatant supernatural incident in the presence of police officers, government officials, highlights the inability of the state to fully protect and provide for its citizens. It also further casts Peggy as helpless in her attempts to protect her family. The officers' response exemplifies this. They dismissively tell her, "Well, not much we can do about that." They tell her the most they can do is file an incident report and stand by it if anyone questions it. Peggy answers: "A report? Oh, that's brilliant. Every problem I have there's another bloody report to fill out." Her remark serves as a reminder of her socioeconomic vulnerability and the shortcomings of government to actually serve its citizens. The solutions to problems are less focused on humans and more on adding to the power of government.

POSSESSION OR HOAX?

At first, Janet's possession appears to be a case more of multiple personalities than demonic possession. Janet cries out in her nightmare, "Help, stop it!" This wakes her sister Margaret. Janet continues, saying, "This is my house!" She alternates between her regular, childlike voice and a deeper, more masculine inflection. The voice accuses Janet of trespassing. As Margaret watches this exchange, it is easy to believe that Janet is having a nightmare and recreating the voices from it. Margaret, however, then hears an external, older, male voice whisper, "This is my house." The voice turns out to be that of Bill Wilkins, the former occupant of the house, who died of a brain hemorrhage in the armchair in the living room. It is later revealed that Bill is not, in fact, the demonic entity; rather, his possession of Janet was used as a disguise for the demonic entity to wreak havoc. His presence yields another purpose: to protect Janet.

The real entity possessing Janet can project illusions to the family. While staying across the street, Billy hears the front doorbell ringing. Believing it to be the neighbors' dog that has been trained to do that when it needs to be let out, Bill wakes up only to find that the dog is growling by the back door. When he opens it, the dog suddenly morphs into the figure from his toy, the Crooked Man. It sings: "There was a crooked man. He walks a crooked mile. The crooked man stepped forth and rang the crooked bell and thus his crooked soul spiraled into a crooked hell." The voice gets louder, and it approaches the family in the living room; they see it is actually a possessed Janet saying these words. She continues her verse, "Murdered his crooked family and laughed a crooked laugh." The grate then flies off the fireplace and almost impales the neighbor's husband, a stand-in for a father figure to the Hodgsons.

The possession is fueled by her father's absence and acts on the instability of the family in the wake of it. The supernatural events begin soon after Peggy's husband leaves the family for a new one. As Ed remarks, "They [spirits] like to kick you when you're down." Before leaving the family, the father took all the music from the home. The demon twists the "Crooked Man" rhyme and tauntingly sings it to the family. Similarly, the entity haunting Lorraine acts on her fear of the absence of the husband and father, Ed. Valak's name is seen spelled out throughout the Warrens' home: along the wall behind the breakfast table and in wood blocks behind Lorraine in the study. Lorraine, too, becomes susceptible to its influence in being consumed by the disturbing vision it gives her of Ed's death. Not only would his death mean the loss of her husband, but also of the father of their daughter.

When Ed and Lorraine arrive, they attempt to restore balance to the family through creating a sanctuary of sorts for the family. Lorraine speaks one-on-one to Janet, using her own experience as an alienated child to try to connect with her and get her to open up. Janet admits: "I'm just so tired. I can't sleep here. I used to go to the medic room at school, and they'd let me sleep there because I was so worn out. But now I can't even do that. Everyone's afraid of me. I got no friends. No place I can go to. It makes me feel like I'm not normal." Lorraine challenges the concept of normal and relates her own personal story of the first time she saw an angel, saying that no one believed her own experiences with the supernatural until she found someone who did. Although her story is meant to reassure Janet that the supernatural is, in fact, a natural part of life, it also clearly differs from Janet's own experiences in that Lorraine experienced an angelic force of good, whereas Janet suffers from demonic possession. Lorraine tells Peggy that she and the kids "need to be a family again," so she and Ed will stay with them. Ed buys an Elvis record, a favorite of the children, and when the record player turns out to be broken, he picks up the father's guitar and starts playing "Unchained Melody." He likens the spirit haunting Janet to a bully, telling her siblings that they must stand up to it. As he sings "I can't help falling in love with you," he stares devotionally at Lorraine, who stands in the doorframe clad in all white, her presence and his words casting a symbolically angelic presence in the home.

MATERNAL SAVIOR

Just as Peggy is struggling to maintain control over and protect her family, Lorraine struggles to protect her family as well. The opening scene of the film is situated in the Amityville house as Lorraine enters a trance to determine if Ronald DeFeo Jr. was influenced by a demonic entity or his own anger in the murder of his family and then himself. She astral projects through the house, acting as he did while he enacted each murder. She looks in the mirror, and the viewer sees DeFeo's reflection in it; she feels that DeFeo was overcome by guilt when he realized the horrible murders he committed. In this moment, Lorraine's body becomes an unstable body. No longer her own, she is able to take on the form of both man and woman. By doing so, this scene can be read as queering Lorraine's otherwise heterosexual body. Because it is met with horror, the film problematizes queer bodies as ones that defy traditional gender binaries. For Lorraine to take on the mind of a man is abhorrent, something that society feared so much that it restricted women's activities and literacy.

This fluid state simultaneously allows her to be more receptive to spirits. She sees a spirit who leads her to the family basement; like in the first film, this is a site of memory, as it is filled with artifacts and furniture. The spirit shows her a mirror that is covered over with a cloth, an image that is like a caricature of a ghost. The cloth drops, and the reflection of an evil nun appears first behind her and then in front of her. It strangles her and then shows her the vision of her husband's neck snapping; it is this vision that forces Lorraine back into her original body. The choice of the nun's shape threatens Lorraine's faith in the Catholic Church as well as subverting the maternal image of a nun by replacing it with something unholy. If her psychic abilities are gifts from God, then the choice of the nun's form is meant as a warning.

The demon invades the Warrens' personal home. While sitting around the breakfast table, the name Valak is spelled out in letters along the windowsill. In another scene, Lorraine sits reading her Bible as her daughter Judy beads. Judy senses a spirit in the hallway and points to the figure of the nun at the end of the hall. Lorraine enters Ed's study to confront it and a recording of a children's choir singing "Hark! The Herald Angels Sing" plays as the demon's shadow walks along the wall to the painting of its likeness. The demon then transports both it and Lorraine back into the Amityville basement. Outside of the trance, Lorraine feverishly writes the demon's name in her Bible. The demon's name, however, was right next to her the entire time, spelled out in letters on the bookcase beside her: Valak. These two scenes emphasize Lorraine's inability to see the obvious due to fear. In targeting the Warrens in their own home, the distinct divide between the supernatural and domestic that they were able to maintain in the first film is no more; instead, the second film deeply intertwines the Warrens' personal and professional realms to heighten the atmosphere of fear and suspense.

These visions are designed to frighten. Afraid that continuing their paranormal investigations will lead to Ed's untimely demise, Lorraine tells him that they have to stop, at least temporarily. She hesitates to accept the priest's request for she and Ed to help Janet, even after hearing the tape of the possessed Janet:

> ED: I told him we'd talk about it.
> LORRAINE: There's nothing to talk about.
> ED: Honey, you heard him. . . . There's never been a family we've refused to
>   help.
> LORRAINE: I had a vision in Amityville. It was the same one I had seven years
>   ago. I had a premonition of your death. . . . It's a warning. If we keep doing
>   this, you're going to die.[8]

Ed, however, is not deterred, instead reminding her that her visions are a gift from God, "and if God is showing you my death, then He's doing it for a reason. Maybe you're meant to prevent it from happening. Come on, we don't run from fights." The exchange between the two showcases the Warrens as a positive marriage, with Ed acting in a supportive role. Ed's words are intended to be a rallying cry for his wife; however, even afterward, she is still filled with the original fear of his death. She is unable to sense any entity, saying: "My heart is telling me to believe them [the Hodgsons]. I heard that voice with my own ears, but all I can sense is their own fear. I can't seem to see beyond that." It is not only the family's fear that she senses, but it is her own fear as well. It is not until she and Ed are away from the house and the family, on the train to the airport, that she is able to receive a vision that reveals the reality of Janet's possession and haunting. For her restored abilities to appear while on a train, a moving vehicle, as opposed to the grounded house is symbolic as the train is a mechanical body constantly in motion, while a house is fixed.

In her vision, she is back at the house, and Bill's spirit is sitting in the armchair in the living room. He admits: "I come here to see my family, but they're not here now. I think I'd like to go now. I can't. . . . It wants her. It almost has her." Up until this point, it was believed that he was the demonic entity possessing Janet. In reality, it is a darker presence that was trying to claim Janet. In choosing to remain behind, Bill's spirit acts as both disguise and protector for the girl. This positions Bill's spirit in a type of grandfatherly role, acting as a shield to delay the demon. Through inhabiting Janet's body, he likewise acts in blurring her binary body between male and female. Although not as extreme as Regan's unstable body in *The Exorcist*, Janet displays this instability of the bodily barrier through her teleportation around the house in addition to her changing voice from her higher-pitched, feminine voice to a lower, masculine one. In the climax of her possession, Janet's face takes on qualities similar to Regan's as well, with yellow eyes, unusually pale skin, and dark veins under her eyes and mouth. Overall, however, Janet's body is not subjected to the extreme that Regan's body was. Although Regan and Janet are raised by single mothers, Regan's mother is clearly wealthy, while Janet's mother struggles financially. Peggy is told that telling her story to the public is her best chance at getting help, forcing her and her family to become spectacles in the public eye. In doing so, the Hodgson family are exposed to another type of possession: media. Some support their claims, including the police officers who first investigated the home; however, others doubt it as a hoax and an excuse to get better housing. Janet and Margaret are interviewed on camera, during which Janet enters a state of possession. The family is thus stripped of their privacy and made open to the external

Lorraine uses the knowledge of the demon's identity to send him back to hell and save Ed (Patrick Wilson) and Janet (Madison Wolfe). © Warner Bros. Pictures.

opinions and influences of the media. The result perpetuates the hauntings by the demonic, purposely blinding Lorraine's sight so that she is unable to read the situation for herself. Bill also gives Lorraine a clue as to how to break the demon's hold: its name. Lorraine then sees the image of the demonic nun a second time and realizes that it took on the form of the nun to attack her faith. An embodiment of her fear, Lorraine must confront the demon that has haunted her. She realizes that by taking the form of a nun, it led Lorraine to question her God-given ability. She finds Ed and Janet upstairs in the house. A possessed Janet tries to kill herself by impaling herself on a broken tree stump in the shape of an enlarged stake coming out of the ground, a very phallic image; dying in this way is an act that hints at the lack of a father figure being the cause of her possession, with Janet willing to sacrifice herself to be reunited with the masculine presence. Ed catches her before she can, acting as a surrogate father figure to protect her. Lorraine tries to help the pair, but the demon pushes her against the wall in a pseudocrucifixion pose. She yells: "Your name gives me dominion over you, demon! And I do know your name. You are Valak, the defiler, the profane, the marquis of snakes! In the name of the Father and of the Son and of the Holy Spirit, I condemn you back to hell!" She is able to remember the demon's true name because of an earlier vision in which she demanded it tell her its name; she then wrote it down in her Bible. Not only that, but her own words also possess the power to do what Ed could not: exorcise the demon. No ritual is required.

Lorraine costumed as female Jesus looking at those she healed. © Warner Bros. Pictures.

She expresses her resumptive agency as mother and wife, and it is her power that ultimately saves Janet and Ed. She likewise assumes the traditional masculine role in eradicating the demon from the house, saving the man in distress instead of the traditional woman in distress. The positioning of her body, levitating in the air against the wall, lends to her a Jesus image, combined with her all-white outfit. Lorraine later tells Ed, "You saved her [Janet]" to which Ed refuses to take credit. He points out that that Lorraine was the one who saved them both. His refusal to take credit and instead acknowledge her role add to the positive depiction of their marriage, with the pair acting more as partners instead of in traditional roles.

After Janet is freed from Valak's hold, she, Ed, Lorraine, and Peggy sit with the ambulance. Ed gifts his cross to Janet, and the pair share a fatherly moment:

> ED: This has kept me safe since I was a kid. I want you to have it, and when you grow up, you find someone who needs it, you give it to them.
> JANET: I'm so lucky. You say one person can change everything. But I've got two.

Janet recognizes the fatherly influence of Ed just as the cross symbolizes the fatherly influence of God. The "two" people who changed everything for Janet are not Ed and Peggy; they are Ed and Lorraine. Peggy is overlooked in the scene; instead, the nuclear pair of Ed and Lorraine are the focus. In doing so, the film undercuts Peggy's maternal role and casts her aside to preference the mother-father pair of the Warrens.

Although they are able to cleanse the demonic from the homes, the Warrens are not able to expel the socioeconomic influences that consistently haunt the families. The cracked walls, lack of financial and government support, and instable paternal presence remain even after the uplifting music ends and credits roll. The films thus end truly unresolved, hinting that these ever-present stresses could open the family to more supernatural strife. The films do, however, shift from the traditional possession film whereby the F/father saves to one that posits the maternal as savior and salvation.

CHAPTER 6

Traumatic Motherhood
The Babadook

The films discussed so far are ones in which mothers are idealized, criticized, and even dismissed. Despite the pressures and challenges these women face, they are all ones who accept their maternal role without question. *The Babadook* goes against this happy acceptance by showing the mother to be one who is seemingly averse to her child given the trauma she carries from her husband's death. The film directly critiques the ideal of the happy, nurturing mother by instead depicting a constant battle between grief, trauma, and the performance of motherhood.

Amelia Vanek is a character marked by trauma. The movie opens with the night her husband Oskar died in a car crash that she survived; the two were on their way to the hospital for her to give birth. It is this memory that is repeatedly played in her mind and the grief from that experience that defines her. As Adolfo Aranjuez writes: "The film is littered with evidence of Amelia's ongoing grief. She still wears her wedding ring. She refuses to talk about the events surrounding Oskar's death and reprimands their son when he does so. And she hoards Oskar's belongings in the basement of their three-story house, kept from prying eyes under lock and key" (123). Also occupying her attention is her son, Samuel, and later, the Babadook, a supernatural creature that inhabits her home. Both compete for possession of Amelia's love and attention, and both disrupt the traditional order of the family to influence and reshape her maternal identity. Her relationship with the two serves to contest the masculine role in her life since the desired masculine,

115

her husband, is taken away from her and replaced by the undesirable, her son, Samuel. The Babadook's possession emphasizes this reality for Amelia, and she is forced to choose between living with a reenactment of her husband or the tumultuous reality of her son.

In an interview with Paul Risker for the *Quarterly Review of Film and Video*, director Jennifer Kent addresses the inspiration for the movie, commenting:

> I feel that it is very important as a person to face the difficulties in oneself and in one's own life—to face the shadow side. I am always fascinated by people who don't do that, and who manage to suppress everything. So that was the entry point for me. I thought: what would it be like to follow a character who really suppresses some of the terrible events in her life, and then has to face them. (14)

For the mother-son duo, that shadow side is grief and the loss of a husband and father. From the beginning, Kent depicts Amelia as a character who attempts to suppress the trauma of Oskar's death. Samuel also struggles with his own unresolved emotions in not having a father and the obligation to fulfill the masculine role in his absence. Caruth writes that the story of trauma is "a kind of double telling, the oscillation between a *crisis of death* and the correlative *crisis of life*: between the story of the unbearable nature of an event and the story of the unbearable nature of its survival" (7, emphasis original). *The Babadook* illustrates Caruth's concept of trauma from the opening scene of the film, with Amelia's flashback dream of the night she was involved in the car accident resulting in the death of her husband before transitioning into the reality of her waking. The camera faces Amelia as she rapidly breathes while going into labor. There is a sharp noise, Amelia is thrown, and darkness and glass shards line the scene while she is tossed. She then turns to her husband, and we see that she is in a car. A white light glows, the camera comes closer to her face, and she falls backward onto her bed.

It becomes clear that it was a dream, a flashback to the night Oskar died and Samuel was born. We do not see the act of Oskar's death in the scene; rather, his death is implied through his absence in her waking. The scene contains elements reminiscent of Caruth's research on trauma, which draws on Freud:

If *fright* is the term by which Freud defines the traumatic effect of not having been prepared in time then the trauma of the nightmare does not simply consist in the experience *within* the dream, but *in the experience of waking from it*. It is the experience of *waking into consciousness* that, peculiarly, is identified with the reliving of the trauma . . . the very *waking itself* that constitutes the surprise: the fact not only of the dream but of having passed beyond it . . . the trauma consists not only in having confronted death but in *having survived, precisely, without knowing it*. What one returns to in the flashback is not the incomprehensibility of one's near death, but the very incomprehensibility of one's own survival. (64, emphasis original)

In waking from the dream, Amelia acquaints herself with the reality of the home she shares with her young son. In doing so, she awakens to the absence of her husband and the reality of another, more undesirable, male presence: her overbearing, demanding son. The opening scene offers the viewers a glimpse into the trauma Amelia copes with, with the flashback, which recurs, to the night she and Oskar were involved in the car accident on their way to the hospital for her to give birth to their son; Amelia and the child survive, but she relives the moment that her husband was killed over and over again in both dreams and reality.

Mother-Son Relationship

The scene switches from the nightmare to her bedroom, showing that she experiences a falling-like sensation as she gradually wakes up to Samuel repeatedly crying, "Mom!" He tells her that he "had that dream again," a parallel to Amelia's own, only his involves a monster in his room, whereas hers involves an internal monster: her grief.[1] She goes into his room and checks for monsters while he clings to her waist, a symbolic desire to return to the womb that indicates his level of fear and worry. She reads him *The Three Little Pigs*, an appropriate story given that it also involves a creature whose aim is to destroy houses to prey on its habitants. Samuel asks, "Did they really kill the wolf?" When his mother replies that they did, he assures her: "I'll kill the monster when it comes. I'll smash its head in." His questions and responses point to a very dark mindset for such a young child. He understands what it is to kill and adamantly admits that he will do so when

Amelia (Essie Davis) and Sam (Noah Wiseman) look for monsters in the night. © IFC Films.

the monster appears; his words predetermining the monster as an inevitable evil he must destroy. It also connects with his birth as well since his birth was marked by the violence of the fatal car crash, showing that he was born out of destruction and born to survive.

Amelia attempts to put her son to sleep after finishing this nighttime ritual. He asks her to read the story again. Without objection, she complies. He falls asleep in bed with his mother, his arms wrapped securely around her neck and tugging at it, while his legs are around her waist, symbolically overwhelming and smothering her. His feet and jaw move, the sounds amplified for the audience to let them hear what Amelia is hearing: every motion, every sound coming from Samuel. He puts his leg around her waist, and it is this implicitly sexual motion that causes Amelia to separate herself from him in bed. The indication of the blurring between son and husband becomes clear as Samuel invades Amelia's personal space in a manner more fitting a husband than a son.

Samuel is the dominant, needy child who navigates between the roles of masculine protector and small child, while Amelia is the passive, submissive mother who struggles to have domestic space for herself. Even when she attempts to masturbate, to claim her sexuality and the bed for herself, she is interrupted by Samuel jumping on the bed, channeling her sexual agency back to her role as his mother. Instead of bringing him to his bedroom, she lays him down next to her in bed, sacrificing her personal space to fulfill her role as his mother. In addition to her physical space, Samuel invades Amelia's symbolic space by breaking into the basement and openly displaying photographs of his father. Addressing one of these photographs, he asserts his masculine authority in saying, "Don't worry, Dad, I'll save Mom." When Amelia scolds him for going into the basement, he yells that he has a right to the space and his father's things, reminding her: "He's my father! You don't own him!" And he tells her coworker, "She won't let me have a birthday party, and she won't let me have a dad." His words are possessive, removing ownership of Amelia's emotions toward Oskar and showcasing resentment toward his mother at restricting his control. His actions force Amelia to enter the basement, a domestic space whose position at the base of the house and whose function as a site of repression correlates to the suppression of trauma. It is here that she first sees the outline of the Babadook through the arrangement of some of Oskar's clothing on a wall, a physical manifestation of the horror she attempts to deny.

Samuel consistently demands Amelia's attention throughout the film, reaffirming her role as caretaker and repeatedly shouting "Mom!" to her at the park while she talks to her sister and then later screeching "Momma!" on the car ride back home after injuring himself from jumping from the top of the swing set. His screams on the car ride take on an accusatory tone, associating the pain he feels with her failure to pay attention to him, blaming his injury on her momentary neglect of motherhood. On a car ride home from his cousin's birthday party, in which he pushes his cousin Ruby (Chloe Hurn) out of her own tree house, he squirms in the backseat, screaming, "Mommy . . . Mommy! Mommy!" His piercing cries get louder with each summon. Samuel's increasingly louder demands for his mother's attention are in keeping with the words written in the *Mister Babadook* book: "The more you deny me, the stronger I'll get," a connection that casts Samuel as the monster terrorizing Amelia's life. Amelia stops the car and turns around to face her son, finally voicing her frustrations in shouting, "Why can't you just be normal?" Samuel screams again, thinking that there is a monster in the car, saying, "Get out! Get out!" before having a fit and collapsing, tensed in the fetal position, in the car. His reaction serves to remind Amelia of her motherly role: she grabs her son, taking him from the car to the sidewalk, and, returning to her maternal role, begs with people, "Please help me! There's something wrong with my son."

Amelia, the tired, long-suffering mother, works as a caretaker at a nursing home, while attempting to handle Samuel's mischief. She wears a pale-pink uniform with white stockings and sneakers, an overtly feminine image tied to an occupation most traditionally associated with women and nurturing. She apologizes for his repeated misbehavior and exercises much discipline with him to little avail. Jessica Balanzategui notes that the film portrays Amelia in a sympathetic light, purposely emphasizing Samuel's deviance from a normal child:

> Because we are positioned to identify with Amelia throughout the first half of the film rather than her child—whose motivations and thought-processes are initially obscure to both the audience and his mother—the audience is invited to share in Amelia's exasperation and exhaustion as Samuel keeps her awake each night with his demands to sleep in her bed, even after she dutifully fulfills the ritual of checking the house for monsters. As a result, the audience is also invited to empathize with Amelia's attempts to quash the child's unhealthy fixation with the creature when she insists that "this monster thing has got to stop," that "if the Babadook was real we would see it, right now, wouldn't we," and that "it's just a book, it can't hurt you." (114)

She suppresses her frustration with him to maintain a calm, composed exterior. She defends him even when he is at fault, such as when he gets in trouble for bringing a homemade weapon into school. The principal (Tony Mack) suggests assigning a monitor for Samuel given his troublesome behavior, and Amelia rejects the idea, saying that he "won't cope" and that "he already feels so different." She is in denial that something is wrong with her son and reduces his issues to a lack of "understanding," blaming the institution and not considering that something may, indeed, be wrong with him, her words acting as a projection of her own insecurities.

THE CHILD IN CRISIS

To admit that Samuel needs help would be to further stigmatize her motherhood. She was unable to help her husband and now is faced with possibly being unable to help her son. As a single mother, she is already stigmatized; as a single mother of an unruly and potentially dangerous child, the stigmatization would increase. Austin Riede addresses this marginalization of motherhood:

> Being a single mother of a young child carries another stigma, and being the single mother of a child with what Sam's school principal describes as "sig-

nificant behavioral problems" is a much greater stigma. Throughout the first
half of the film Jennifer Kent relentlessly underscores Amelia's frustration and
her lack of individual agency or identity in the face of her son's behavior. As
she grows more publicly alienated from the other characters in the film, and
from the social institutions such as the school and the police, which offer no
help, the presence of the Babadook continues to grow within her house, as we
see her son embarrass her in public, smash property, endanger other children,
and push his cousin out of a tree-house, breaking her nose. (137)

The principal's refusal to call Samuel by his first name and instead simply
refer to him as "the boy," while only referring to Amelia by her married name,
furthers this stigma by stripping the characters of their individuality beyond
their societal roles. These words are similarly repeated again in the film when
the Babadook assumes Oskar's form, telling Amelia that they can be together
if she brings him "the boy." Both scenes highlight the underlying struggle for
Amelia to truly see Samuel as a "boy," her child, and herself as the parent.

This struggle to understand appropriate parent-child roles is shown when
Amelia gets Samuel ready for school. He wears a magician's cape, top hat, and
gloves; his costuming is more adult, mimicking the role of a magician. The
magic trick is that he gives her a bouquet of flowers. Although seemingly
innocent, the moment becomes inappropriate when he caresses her cheek
with a gloved hand and hugs her close, moaning, "Mmm . . . mmm." His
actions take the scene from an exchange appropriate for a mother and son to
one that is more appropriate for a woman and a man. Another interpretation
of the action is that of a baby touching a mother's cheek; given Samuel's age,
this is also not appropriate. Amelia's reaction to Samuel's inappropriateness is
to repel him away from her and tell him, "Don't do that." Her reaction shows
an awareness of Samuel's inappropriate behavior as well as a moment of her
reinforcing her maternal dominance over her child so as to establish the
proper order of the family. The Babadook later takes on a similar costuming to Samuel in this scene, with a top hat and overcoat that acts as a cape.
Just as she is forced to assert agency in this scene over Samuel, so, too, does
she later reclaim her maternal power to control the monstrous Babadook.

For Amelia, the solution to Samuel's misbehavior is to sedate him, both
metaphorically and physically. Samuel breaks a window in the kitchen with
his homemade catapult, and later, Amelia finds shards of glass like those
from the broken window in her soup. Samuel denies any involvement;

consequentially, he is told to go into the living room to watch his video about magic while she cleans up and cooks them something else. She begs the doctor for sedatives so that they can both sleep in peace instead of being woken up by a supposed monster. That night, Amelia's tone resumes the calm, nurturing one in the following bedtime conversation between she and Samuel:

> SAMUEL: Why don't people like me? . . . Ruby said people don't like me because I'm weird.
>
> AMELIA: Sometimes people say things that aren't true. Just need to take your medicine, get a big sleep, and not worry.
>
> SAMUEL: I don't want you to die.
>
> AMELIA: I'm not going to die for a long time yet.
>
> SAMUEL: Did you think that about my dad before he died?
>
> AMELIA: Just take your pill so you can go to sleep.
>
> SAMUEL: Will these make the Babadook go away?
>
> AMELIA: I think so. You have to promise me you won't mention it again.
>
> SAMUEL: I promise to protect you if you promise to protect me. Then I won't mention it.
>
> AMELIA: I promise to protect you.

Samuel's words hint at a desire to know more about his father and to internalize his grief at not having one. The sequence of his questions, first about his father, then about the Babadook, inherently links the monster's presence with grief and trauma; Amelia's response and her turn to sedatives for Samuel point to repression of that trauma.

This scene shows a change in sympathies toward Samuel. Much as the audience sympathizes with Amelia, we begin to become genuinely concerned for Samuel's well-being and rethink some of his earlier actions as expressions of anxiety instead of unruliness or disobedience. As Riede states:

> In the first half of the film, we are taught to feel what Amelia feels towards Sam: a deep and enduring annoyance. . . . As the roles begin to shift . . . our sympathies lie more and more with Sam, and not only because we see the threat to his life, but we see that he is dealing with it in a child-like but remarkably mature way. He is keeping his promise to protect his mother, despite her becoming the threat from which he needs to protect both of them. (138)

In this scene, Samuel is shown as conscious of how others perceive him and troubled with that knowledge. Not only that, but he shows genuine concern regarding the safety and well-being of his mother, a mature perspective to have for a six-year-old. He does not want to be different. He wants what any child wants: to feel safe and loved.

This desire is echoed when he hides in his cousin Ruby's tree house during her birthday party. Ruby climbs up, dressed in her princess costume, and asserts her authority over him and the space in the following scene:[2]

RUBY: This is my tree house. You're not allowed in here.
SAMUEL: I'm not hurting anybody. . . . Your mom never comes to our house.
RUBY: Mom told Dad she didn't want to go to your house because it's too depressing.
SAMUEL: [In a menacing voice] The Babadook would eat your mom for breakfast. It'd rip her arms off.
RUBY: Shut up! You're not even good enough to have a dad. Everyone else has one, and you don't.
SAMUEL: I do have a dad!
RUBY: Your dad died so he didn't have to be around you . . . and your mom doesn't want you . . . no one wants you.
[Samuel gets up and pushes her out of the tree house. Amelia and the other partygoers all turn their attention toward Samuel and the fallen Ruby.]
SAMUEL: She said I didn't have a dad! She kept saying it!

Ruby's dialogue represents Samuel's own fears regarding his mother's love and the death of his father. She challenges his self-worth and his lack of a nuclear family, claiming it is because he doesn't deserve one. Samuel's own threat to Ruby regarding her mother and the Babadook shows a momentary shift in perspective from the Babadook as monster to the Babadook as a potential surrogate father figure, protecting Samuel from the cruelty of his cousin and aunt.

The action taking place outside is complemented by the one taking place in the kitchen with Amelia and the other mothers. The body language is paralleled between mother and son, with Amelia sitting further away from the mothers and thus detached. Claire (Hayley McElhinney) attempts to include her sister in the group, but it is evident that Amelia's trauma and financial realities prevent her from connecting with the affluent women. One mentions her volunteer work with disadvantaged women, while also complaining about how her motherly duties have left her with no time to go to the gym. Amelia sarcastically comments how the mother must have so much in common with the disadvantaged women. Throughout the scene, the camera highlights Amelia's isolation and social standing as an outsider. Aranjuez explains,

> Amelia is seated alone in the centre of frame; in the complementing shot, Claire and the other mothers are in a row facing her, as though an interview panel. Already, Amelia sticks out, but this is intensified by the contrasts in wardrobe: whereas the other mothers are uniformly donned in black or dark grey, perfectly styled hair worn down, Amelia sports a pink dress under her black coat, untidy hair in a pony-tail. Compounding this, their daughters are all in pink outfits, aligning Amelia with the children's inferior status. (124)

Aranjuez argues that it shows Amelia failing to perform a particular appropriate mode of motherhood. Not only that, it furthers Amelia's isolation: she is financially unstable, the government casts her as a bad mother, and her own sister is unsupportive.

The Monster Unleashed

The film makes the viewer question if there is, in fact, a monster or if the supposed monster is the product of the child's imagination. The music hints at the association between the monster and childhood, with slow, music-box-like tinkling playing in the background when the creature is supposedly around. Amelia discovers thin shards of glass in her soup, similar to those from the windowpane Samuel broke earlier in the film. Samuel automatically tells her, "The Babadook did it, Mom," but the expression on her face says she questions otherwise. After dinner, she sees and hears Samuel scurrying from her bedroom. She enters it to see that photograph of her and Oskar from the basement has been destroyed, with Oskar's face scratched out and Amelia's lower lip and under eyes bloodied. She confronts Samuel:

AMELIA: Do you think this is funny?
[Samuel runs to grab his weapon, and Amelia tries to take it from him.]
AMELIA: Give it to me!
SAMUEL: [Pushes his mother to the ground.] Do you want to die?

There are no consequences for his act of aggression toward his mother, denying Amelia resolution and reaffirming Samuel's control over her. In his room, Samuel straps a weapon to his back and attacks the bureau. The result is that the bureau topples down, and the noise causes Amelia to enter the room. When she does so, she finds Samuel curled up in a fetal position underneath his bed, repeating: "Don't let it in! Don't let it in!" Once again, Amelia's solution to his fears is to bring him into her bed. Her bed thus becomes a site of resignation for her and a symbolic womb. It is there that she attempts to repair her fragmented family by having Samuel occupy Oskar's place, and it is there that Samuel finds the most safety in the comfort of his mother; both interpretations placing the emphasis on other characters, not Amelia herself.

A second version of the *Mister Babadook* book appears after Amelia burns the first one. The original version centered around the monster haunting a little boy and corresponds with Samuel's amplified claims of seeing the monster. This version differs from the original version, however. The pages of the second book are ripped and glued together and feature the monster targeting a woman, not a child. Balanzategui notes the significance of Amelia's reaction toward the books, saying:

> While Amelia initially exercises her parental control over the storybook— taking it from Samuel, ripping it to pieces and throwing it in the rubbish bin—the events depicted in the book overpower her own agency and cleaving to rational frameworks of meaning. That these hauntings are a monstrous amplification of the repetitive, childish phrases and images from the story-book aestheticizes the growing power of the children's culture from which the story emerges. Throughout the film, the various regulatory gatekeepers of the epistemic regimes of adult culture—doctors, teachers, and police offi-cers—are powerless to confront this supernaturally-charged expression of children's culture, for they do not believe in, let alone respect or understand, its existence. (114)

Amelia is made to understand that the monster is real, however. Whereas the first version illustrates a little boy being possessed by the monster, this revised version features a female character possessed by the creature and the lines: "The more you deny, the stronger I get. . . . You start to change when I get in. The Babadook growing right under your skin. Oh come! Come see what's underneath." The lines are alongside images of the Babadook trying to enter the woman. His shadow becomes her shadow, which kills the dog, the boy, and then herself. The book foreshadows Amelia's possession as the more she attempts to pass as "normal," the stronger the hold of the entity. The ripped-up pages provide a preview of her fragmented identity that the possession will disrupt, reshape, and reform.

Soon after reading the second version of *Mister Babadook*, Amelia begins to see outlines of the monster as the book's words manifest themselves around the house. The first time she perceives the creature is by Oskar's clothes hanging on the basement wall, making the connection to Amelia's repressed trauma clear and harkening the Babadook's home in the basement itself. One night, while Samuel is asleep in her bed beside her, she sees the figure of the Babadook enter the room, climb the ceiling, and enter her mouth to possess and stifle her scream. The camera narrows on Amelia's mouth, open wide, imbuing her possession with a sexual tone. The second time the creature possesses Amelia, he taunts her before entering her body. He throws his hat down the chimney, and his coat drops on the floor around a crawling, terrified Amelia. She looks up to see the creature on the ceiling, like an insect. He unsheathes his clawlike hands, the movement sounding like knives, and comes down to her. The viewer never sees the creature in front of Amelia. Instead, the viewer only sees Amelia open her mouth to gasp. The implication is that the creature entered Amelia from behind this time, further emphasizing the sexual tone to the possession. It becomes clear that Samuel's claims of seeing the creature—the monster he promises to kill and protect his mother from—are, in fact, truth and not the product of his imagination; consequently, his attempts to protect his mother and their home can be viewed as trying to assume the traditional protector role in light of his father's absence.

The hauntings Amelia experiences call her motherhood into question through undermining her maternal agency. Her sister alludes to Amelia's financial troubles on the phone, saying, "You can't even pay your own bills," implying that her sister provides financial assistance. The next phone call is the monster who only says, "Baba . . . dook!" That night in the kitchen, Amelia looks around and sees that it is messy, with a sink full of dirty dishes. She sees a roach on the floor coming from underneath the fridge. She moves the fridge and sees a vaginal-shaped crack in the wall where the roaches are coming from, representing her birthing the pestilent possession and associating Samuel's birth with disease and infection. The roaches again appear when she is driving the car, with Samuel seated in the back. She sees the outline of the Babadook in the rearview mirror and hears the creature croak, "Baba . . . dook!" She crashes into another car, the second car crash of the film: the first being the night Oskar died on the way to the hospital for her to give birth. Back at the house, child services knock on the door. During the visit, Samuel relays to them, "I'm a bit tired from the drugs Mother gave me. . . . I'm really tired actually." His use of her formal title—Mother—in the context of giving him bad drugs shows she is failing in her motherly role to protect and care for him.

A possessed Amelia emerges from the basement with Oskar's violin and lies down in her bed with it beside her. Samuel comes up on the other side and puts his hand around her waist in a suggestively romantic gesture to touch his father's violin. Taking ownership over Oskar's memory, she shouts, "Leave it!" She wakes to Samuel whispering on the phone to a neighbor. She takes the phone from him and assures her neighbor: "Samuel's just being very disobedient again. I told him not to call anyone." She emphasizes his disobedience and then addresses him, "I told you not to call anyone, and you deliberately disobeyed me." She takes the phallic butcher knife from the kitchen drawer and cuts the phone cord, an action that literally and symbolically severs the connection between the inside of the house and the outside world, imprisoning Amelia, Samuel, and the monster. As she watches television later that night, she cradles a bloated stomach that is similar to a pregnant belly. She looks over to see a vision of Samuel with a sliced throat and blood down his shirt. This, however, is only a dream. Samuel wakes her up only for her to realize she is holding the butcher knife from the kitchen, suggesting what she might have done in her enchanted sleep state.

CONFRONTING TRAUMA

What's "underneath," for Amelia, as the book suggests, is her trauma. This time, it manifests itself in her rage and hurt toward Samuel as she finally reveals her suffering. She tells him: "Sometimes I just want to smash your head against a brick wall until your fucking brains pop out. . . . You don't know how many times I wished it was you, not him, that had died." She confesses, "I haven't been good since your dad died. . . . I'm sick, Sam." Samuel uses the butcher knife against his mother, stabbing her in the upper thigh

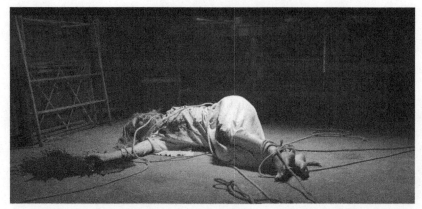

Amelia bound with a symbol of motherhood and freed of the Babadook's influence. © IFC Films.

near her groin. In doing so, he phallically penetrates her and reasserts his authority. Because his birth is tied to the sudden death of Oskar, he also physically opens the traumatic wound.

He traps his mother in the basement, tying her up with rope and strapping her to the floor. Her white nightgown is stained from a struggle between the pair in the kitchen, with blood from where Samuel struck her with the butcher knife; this stain appears near her groin area. The imagery of Amelia in this scene is reminiscent of birth, with Amelia tied to the basement floor with ropes, symbolic of an umbilical cord, and the bloodstain like that of amniotic fluid. He climbs on top of her and caresses her cheek, remarking: "I'm not leaving you. I know you don't love me. The Babadook won't let you. But I love you, Mum. And I always will. . . . You let it in; you have to let it out!" She convulses and vomits black blood; her ropes now loosened and her body mobile, she has reclaimed her motherhood. Samuel hugs her, assured that his mother has returned to her role as the benevolent nurturer.

This is not the end of the film, however; instead, the creature drags Samuel upstairs into Amelia's bedroom onto her bed, attacks him, and shakes the bed—a purposeful choice, considering the bed is a site of procreation and of the problematic relationship between her and Samuel. Riede examines the significance of the bed as the place of confrontation between Amelia and the monster:

> The place of repose and sleep becomes the site Amelia must protect from her darker urges. It is here that she battles the Babadook and claims a decisive victory. The angriest line she delivers in the film is directed not toward her son,

but toward the Babadook, which can of course be read as the force encroach-
ing on her identity, the stigma that threatens to extinguish her entirely from
the race of normal, even if normally stigmatized, human beings. (139)

Oskar's figure then appears, asking Amelia, "What do you want?" The
Babadook then acts out the trauma of the accident in front of her eyes. The
creature purposely shows Oskar's head sliced open, not only repeating what
presumably happened in the accident but symbolically opening Amelia's
mind to the trauma of her past. This repetition is in line with Caruth's theory
on the repetition of the traumatic event: "Repetition, in other words, is not
simply the attempt to grasp that one has almost died but, more fundamentally
and enigmatically, the very attempt *to claim one's own survival*" (64, emphasis
original). Trying to take advantage of Amelia's vulnerability, the creature's
shadow looms larger toward her, but this time, she addresses it, shouting:
"You are nothing. . . . This is my house! You're trespassing in my house! If you
touch my son again, I'll fucking kill you!" Her bedroom as the place where
she ultimately confronts her trauma and the creature is significant since, in
regard to domestic spaces and settings, her bedroom is a rather intimate
place; presumably, it was once her and Oskar's bedroom, and now it is just
her own. It is here that she must come face-to-face with her nightmare, the
loss of her husband, and the overwhelming grief that has rendered her unable
to completely bond with her son.

Rather than allowing her trauma, her grief, to consume her in the form of
the Babadook's shadow, she accepts it, claiming her own survival, in Caruth's
words; in doing so, she accepts her maternal agency, the force of which sends
the Babadook scurrying. The Babadook, however, is not gone forever. The
film makes it clear that the creature is locked in the basement, where Amelia
provides it with earthworms from the garden to eat. It initially confronts
her, causing her to arch backwards. Its groans and screams, sounding like
the noises heard in the background of her opening dream and echoing the
ones from the pivotal confrontation between mother and monster. Rather
than be fearful of it, she is sympathetic, calming it by saying, "It's all right. . . .
Shhh . . . Shhh." The monster is no longer a creature to be feared; instead, it is
one that is scared and needs to be cared for. Her daily visits with it, then, can
be interpreted as a form of supernatural self-care through finally allowing
Amelia to have a space of her own in the house where she can be alone and
confront that which haunts her.

Amelia takes back her house and her son, dispossessing the monster. © IFC Films.

The particular day featured at the end of the film is Samuel's birthday, an occasion Amelia used to not formally acknowledge on the exact day since it coincides with the anniversary of Oskar's death. The Babadook's residence in the basement and the choice of day is fitting as the basement is the site that she originally chose to suppress the trauma of her husband's absence at the beginning of the film. Now she is able to face it and care for it just as she now accepts Samuel for who he is: not a boy she wishes could be normal or wishes died in the crash in place of her husband, but the son who survived and whose existence she celebrates. Riede warns, "The triumph, though, is conditional . . . this happiness is only as real as the Babadook itself, and no more real than the book in which he appears. The stigma of spoiled identity can be managed, sometimes and to some extent, but it does not go away" (140). Although the movie ends with Amelia smiling as she cradles Samuel in her arms, the gesture is one that she formerly used when picking up the family dog, Bugsy, making one question if she truly loves Samuel for who he is or if it is more about what he represents: someone to give her attention.

"You let it in; you have to let it out." Samuel tells his mother this during her exorcism. But grief and trauma are emotions a person can never truly get rid of, only manage, just like the Babadook is a monster the characters cannot rid themselves of but instead have to live with.[3] It is unclear if Amelia is truly happy at the end of the film or if her smile and embrace are like how she watched late-night television, trancelike and as a form of escapism, only an act, now in her new maternal performance.

CHAPTER 7

The Devil's Promise
The Witch

The terror of motherhood is a common trope in the horror genre, with women in horror films required to suffer through any number of abject fears in hope of any type of survival. The worst of these horrors is that a child would become what the mother fears the most: one who moves away from her, turns against her, and rejects her upbringing. It is this fear that is made manifest in Robert Egger's 2015 film *The Witch* as a mother watches her daughter turn slowly toward the devil to become a witch.

No other region in the United States is more synonymous with the concept of the witch than New England. Early New England was a region ripe to cultivate witchcraft accusations. Having migrated from England to seek religious freedom, Puritan settlers hoped to find an ideal setting to exercise their faith; instead, they were greeted with a landscape filled with threats that allowed "New England" and "witchcraft" to become words that are closely tied together. Throughout much of the early New England period of the seventeenth and early eighteenth centuries, witchcraft become a prominent issue, with accounts telling of afflicted bodies of the supposed witchcraft victims and the allegedly abnormal bodies of the accused, who themselves became victims of a continuing hysteria.

This history is what the film borrows for its premise. The film heavily draws from historical documents of early New England witchcraft for plot and dialogue. *The Witch* is about a family who, due to the father's unwavering religious convictions, is banished from the community. They are then forced to rebuild a home and life for themselves out near the woods. Their new life is quickly plagued with diseased crops, grief, and suspicions of witchcraft. William, the father and patriarch of the family, struggles to maintain order and control in the wake of such events only to ultimately become a victim to his own pride. His actions damn his family and act as the catalyst for the eldest daughter, Thomasin, to transform into a witch.

PURITAN MODES OF WOMANHOOD

The image of the witch has been demonized throughout history and in popular culture. The witch is thought to be the cause of socioeconomic failings and strife within a family. After all, it is easier to blame the supernatural than the natural. When discussing the figure of the witch in film, Creed writes: "She is thought to be dangerous and wily, capable of drawing on her evil powers to wreak destruction on the community. The witch sets out to unsettle boundaries between the rational and irrational, symbolic and imaginary. Her evil powers are seen as part of her 'feminine' nature; she is closer to nature than man and can control forces in nature such as tempests, hurricanes and storms" (76).

This cinematic archetype draws from real-life inspiration. Historically, women proved themselves as not always adhering to the Puritan ideal of the passive, submissive woman. Stacey Schiff provides an overview of some of these women who did not conform:

> Women too had troubled New England since its founding: they claimed starring roles as heretics and rebels. Beginning with Ann Hutchinson, the charismatic leader who encouraged women to walk out of sermons and who disrupted church doctrine, they had been speaking their minds, otherwise known as disturbing the peace. At her 1640 trial, Ann Hibbins cited the Old Testament, a text she claimed exhorted husbands to heed their wives. She also took the opposite tack; sixteen years earlier, she refused in court to answer her accusers on the grounds that God demanded the silence of women. (142)

Despite these instances of women expressing empowerment, it should be noted that women in New England still had no political rights. Yet, "officially voiceless, she nonetheless found plenty of ways to make herself heard and demonstrated a vaulting need to speak her mind. In legal records she hectors, shrieks, quarrels, scolds, rants, rails, tattles, and spits" (Schiff 142). Women may have been politically disempowered, but they could still upset order and control.

Indeed, such behavior would be in opposition to Puritan ideals of women. Through being passive and submissive, women were likewise expected to be silent, chaste, and obedient. The Puritan female "was a sterling amalgam of modesty, piety, and tireless industry. She spoke neither too soon nor too much. She read her Scripture twice daily. Her father was her prince and judge; his authority was understood to be absolute. She deferred to him as she would to the man she would marry, in her early twenties" (Schiff 131). To elaborate on this depiction, Schiff continues: "Women did not speak in meeting, demurely of impudently. The fine for interrupting a minister was five pounds or two hours on the block" (83). In other words, the ideal Puritan female was just that: an ideal, an image not easily replicated in reality; rather, these unrealistic standards would give rise to the relationship between women and witchcraft.

From Puritanism to Witchcraft

Thomasin's face is what starts and ends the film. The opening scene shows the family anxiously kneeling before the community's governing body, who demand an answer for William's perceived heresy. They ask William, "Must you continue to dishonor the laws of the Commonwealth? Of the Church? With your prideful deceit?" Although his exact crimes are not revealed, the context implies that it is refusal to conform to religious standards. He replies, "I cannot be judged by false Christians for I have done nothing save preach Christ through the Gospel." Forced to submit to her father's will, Thomasin must also suffer the consequences of banishment from the community and "from [the] plantation's liberties." She is the last to leave the hearing, showing her reluctance to follow her earthly father. In the end, however, she pledges herself to a different, albeit unholy, father in signing the devil's book and becoming a witch. She is transformed from the silent, anxious, submissive daughter at the start to a laughing, naked, free woman.

At first, the two main women in the house—Thomasin and her mother, Katherine—embody ideals of Puritan womanhood. Katherine gazes lovingly and admiringly at William as the family prays before beginning construction

Thomasin (Anya Taylor-Joy) waits for the court's verdict about her father and family.
© A24studio.

on their new homestead. She breastfeeds baby Samuel, the child she presumably gave birth to on the new family farm, while Mercy (Ellie Grainger)
silently dips candles at her mother's feet. The scene is procreative, with
Katherine nurturing her son and Mercy dipping candles into wax, which
are symbolic of mother's milk and semen. It is as though it is taken from a
painting of pure, womanly goodness. Intercut with these images are those of
William and sons working in the fields, harvesting the crop. The two pairings,
with the women dutifully working in the house as the men tend to the fields,
present a brief moment of a unified, seemingly happy family.

Before these actions unfold, however, there is another one that takes place:
Thomasin's confession. She kneels in prayer with her eyes raised upward as
though directly addressing the audience. Her confession starts as the aforementioned scenes play out, with her voice narrating the background:

> I have confessed I've lived in sin. I've been idle in my work, disobedient to my
> parents, neglectful of my prayer. I have, in secret, played upon my Sabbath.
> . . . And broken every one of Thy commandments in thought. . . . I know I
> deserve the shame and everlasting hellfire, but I beg Thee, for the sake of Thy
> Son, forgive me. Show me mercy. Show me that light.

Katherine (Kate Dickie) as the Puritan ideal of motherhood. © A24studio.

Her confession also acts to question whether or not she could, in fact, be a witch. Her words are a contrast to the pillar of Puritanical womanhood that is Katherine by showing her struggle with faith. The specific parts of her confession also act as omens for what is to befall the family: Mercy and Jonas (Lucas Dawson) turn idle and play instead of working, William steals Katherine's silver chalice, and Thomasin is falsely accused of the crime, Thomasin kills her mother, and ultimately, Thomasin chooses to worship another god.

Aviva Briefel notes the progression of Thomasin's transformation into a witch. Up until the final scene, when the audience actually sees Thomasin conjure Black Philip (Daniel Malik) and sign the devil's book, the film teases the viewers with the question of whether or not Thomasin could actually be a witch. Briefel writes: "Thomasin's transformation—subtle at first, extreme in the end—closely follows the stages of possession that could supposedly befall young Puritan women. According to John Demos in his landmark study on witchcraft, *Entertaining Satan*, an early warning sign was of a woman becoming 'anxiously preoccupied with her spiritual condition'" (158). The movie further hints at the association between Thomasin and witchcraft through the organization of the proceeding scenes. After Thomasin's confession, Katherine tasks her with taking care of baby Samuel. She plays a game with him outside to entertain him. This choice is keeping with the confession in regard to her playfulness and deviation from rigid faith. The game she chooses is peekaboo, a purposeful choice because it involves looking and hiding from the other player, similar to Thomasin's unstable faith.[1] She closes her eyes and finds Samuel has disappeared. The next scene reveals a hooded witch carrying the child into the woods. Inside her cottage, she is revealed to be an old, naked woman (Bathsheba Garnett). She caresses Samuel's body, holding a long, narrow knife close to his genitals. She grinds up the removed body parts, and the sounds turn to whacking as clots of tissue and blood are smeared across her body. The ritual regresses the physical child to that of seeds used to regenerate the witch's body. In doing so, it inverts the model of Christian motherhood while also presenting two maternal archetypes: the creator (Katherine) and destroyer (witch).

Katherine also increasingly defies the Puritan ideal of womanhood. She openly describes their home as a "hovel" and criticizes the family, saying: "What is amiss in this fam? It's not natural." William dismisses her concerns and diminishes her grief, stating: "I fear thou dost look too much upon this affliction. We must turn our thoughts toward God. . . . He hath never taken a child from us. Not a one, Kate. . . . We have been ungrateful of God's love." She blames him for the family's problems, saying, "You've cursed this family." To William, however, God has "humbled" the family. She continues to question him:

> KATHERINE: Was not Christ led into the wilderness by the devil? We should never have left the plantation.
> WILLIAM: That damaged church . . . what need we, silver chalices?
> KATHERINE: Listen to me. Our daughter has begot the sin of womanhood. She's old enough. She must leave.
> WILLIAM: 'Twas not her fault.
> KATHERINE: Our children have been like savages. How oft have I begged and begged thee to take Samuel to baptism? Our son is in hell! . . . Our corn is trash!
> WILLIAM: We cannot go back to that church!
> KATHERINE: We will starve!

William's references to "silver chalices" points to Katherine's own silver cup that he traded for traps. Although he belittles the worth of the silver cup, the silver cup is actually valuable and "contrasts sharply with the meager life they now lead, cut off from the life of relative luxury the family has left behind by coming to New England in the first place. The material value of the cup also suggests a luxury that, for those trying to abandon the alleged excesses of Catholicism, would hold a fraught meaning for Puritans" (Briefel 11–12). Although Katherine can be seen as materialistic in her concern, she is actually realistic about the family's situation. She not only questions her husband; she commands him and finds fault with his actions and inaction. She blames him for the family's lack of religious morality and the spiritual state of their children. Likewise, she implicitly associates Thomasin's adolescence with sin and the cause of Samuel's disappearance.

FERTILE POWER

On the surface, Thomasin is not responsible for Samuel's disappearance. However, in choosing to lay the child down in the open, with the woods visible in the background, she unknowingly exposes him to danger. Although stolen through supernatural means, the blame is put on Thomasin as he was put in her care; by losing him, she shares the symbolic burden of losing a child. At the same time, she is navigating being a child herself, positing her status as a young woman in flux. She likewise exposes the family to the witch of the woods in looking away from her brother, even in jest.

Soon after, the family experiences signs of witchcraft through attacks on their crops and livestock as well as changes in characters' behavior. Katherine seemingly goes against Puritan womanhood in making noise: she audibly cries out of grief, constantly scolds Thomasin, and doubts her husband. The corn is diseased, both the phallic corncob and the fertile ear, foreshadowing the threat of witchcraft spreading through the family. The eggs in the hen house are not viable either. A chicken egg contains an almost fully formed, bloody chick, symbolizing the death of the baby Samuel in order to refertilize and renew the witch's body. The traps are unable to ensnare any animals, and it becomes clear that the family may not survive. Blood is found in the goat's milk while Thomasin milks it, tainting the source of nourishment for the family while also symbolizing Thomasin's own fertility as a threat to the family. The blood in the milk is like menstrual blood. What contaminates the milk is like Thomasin's own womanly body tainting the family structure by tempting her brother as well as threatening Katherine's own status as the female in power.

In targeting the family's food source, the witch forces them to turn to the woods and thus fully ensnares and emasculates them. Although the family forbade entering the woods, William and Caleb (Harvey Scrimshaw) enter it to look for food. William tells Caleb: "Our harvest cannot last the winter. We must catch our food if we cannot grow it. We will conquer this wilderness; it will not consume us." His choice of words is purposeful as his use of "consume" implies food and hunger, as well as spiritually. In the woods, he asks his father about the nature of sin. He becomes clearly anxious, saying: "And if I died, if I died this day, I know even in my heart, my sins are not pardoned. And if God will not hear my prayers, tell me!" William fails to reassure and explain theology to his son and, in doing so, fails in his role as the family's religious authority. They spot a hare, and despite staring right at them, they miss the shot. The hare represents masculine reproduction as well as the wilderness; in failing to kill it, William's masculinity and authority are undermined. The gun, a tool of man and technology, is shown as inadequate against the wild, untamed woods.

The association between fertility and the failings of the family homestead connect to history. Although women were expected to be passive and submissive, they were held responsible for many of the socioeconomic failings of the new community:

> Puritan belief made it easy to hold women responsible for the failures of the emerging economic system. Discontent, anger, envy, malice, and pride were understandable responses to the stresses of the social and economic change. Yet the clergy's repeated descriptions of these responses as sins against the hierarchal order of Creation, and their associations of women with these sins and with the Devil, encouraged the conviction among men that if anyone were to blame for their troubles it was the daughters of Eve. (Karlsen 217)

Carol F. Karlsen adds: "Sexual tensions also fostered witchcraft accusations, and these too were endemic to the social arrangements of colonial New England. . . . In requiring women's sexual and economic dependence, they were compelled to support women in that dependence" (217). Puritans "stamped the witch as guilty of interfering with the natural processes of life and death" (Karlsen 141). Women were expected to maintain order, and so for women to be witches is not that far of a stretch given their abilities to "transform milk into cheese and thread into lace . . . coax pudding from dry moss," banal activities that nonetheless demonstrate metamorphic capabilities (Schiff 143).

This evidence of witchcraft has overt ties to fertility. This emphasis on fertility is shown in the relationship between Katherine and Thomasin. Katherine is portrayed as visibly older than her eldest daughter with sharply angled features and hair that is always hidden under a bonnet. Thomasin stands in contrast to her mother in respect to age and beauty. Caleb gazes upon her breasts as she sleeps, depicting her as a temptress. Her hair is blonde and bright, whereas Katherine's is darker and more muted. Thomasin's hair becomes increasingly looser throughout the film, with only a slight glimpse of it at the start of the film and it fully loosened at the end, as opposed to Katherine's, whose hair is securely hidden until her death. Katherine calls Thomasin a "slut" and screams that she took her family from her.

The witch spells Katherine to believe that her two sons—Samuel and Caleb—have returned from the grave to embrace her. Caleb appears holding Samuel and returns her silver chalice. The following conversation takes place:

> CALEB: Mother, we have longed to see you so. . . . We would see you oft, Mother, would that please you?
> KATHERINE: Aye.
> CALEB: I have brought a book for you, Mother. Will you look at it with me?
> KATHERINE: Aye. One moment now. Samuel's hungry.

She takes what she believes to be Samuel in her arms and bares her breast for him to feed and laughs in delight as she feels him latch on. In reality, it is the witch's familiar that she feeds and who pecks away at her breast, her motherhood perverted to feed an unholy creature. As this dialogue takes place, Mercy and Jonas see the older witch feeding from one of the goats. She is naked and cries out. It is from the family's goat that the witch feeds, literally and symbolically preying upon the family. This is in contrast to the interior scene of Katherine breastfeeding what she imagines to be the babe, Samuel; however, it is, in fact, a crow pecking at her breast that she feeds with her blood and milk. The imagery subverts the image of the nurturing mother with that of the witch as Katherine enthusiastically feeds the witch's familiar and the witch's power.

The witch not only feeds on baby Samuel but on Caleb as well. Through targeting the boys, the witch ensures the end of the family line. Caleb's possession has ties to issues of sexuality and acts to further destabilize the family. Caleb and Thomasin enter the woods to attempt to provide food for their family so that Thomasin will not be sent away.[2] He holds his father's shotgun, the imagery meant to posit him as a surrogate patriarch in the wake of his father's failure to provide for the family. In the woods, he spots the hare and attempts to go after it; instead, he wanders deeper into the woods to the witch's cottage. He encounters the witch in the woods, now transformed into a beautiful woman (Sarah Stephens) with a mossy dress and plump lips. He walks closer to her, and she caresses his face and draws him in for a kiss.

Upon discovering their son lost, William means to go after him in the dark woods. Katherine cries, "You have no gun, William!" And she calls him a fool for believing that he could enter the woods without one. Her outspokenness undermines William's patriarchal authority. He reveals that he was the one who took her silver cup to sell for food and pelts; in doing, the exchange can be read as a betrayal of his Christian identity, lying to his wife in order to avoid her ire. Katherine exclaims: "I knew you were false . . . you've broken God's covenant. You're a liar! And you've lost another child! You cannot escape the woods. . . . Will you damn all your family to death?" Her speech reads as a series of accusations against her husband, and her proclamation that he cannot escape the woods shows the power of the woods on the family.

When he emerges from the woods, it is Thomasin who discovers him naked outside in the rain. There are cuts on his arms and shoulders plus bites around his mouth, suggesting an inhuman attack. Katherine and Thomasin care for him by using a knife to bleed him from his temple. Using the knife, they bleed the infection the witch wrought upon him by focusing on his mind in an attempt to release the poison. A rotten apple is released from his mouth, a manifestation of inverse fertility. Earlier, he lied to his mother to protect his father by saying he and his father went searching for apples in the valley to try to cheer her in her grief over Sam. Because of this, the rotted apple in his possession can be seen as a mockery of the family's fragile happiness. The apple also ties to Genesis, and its connection with his screams of "My bones! My stomach!" situate the sinfulness of Creation in the corporeal by marking his body as a sinful one. He prays: "My Lord, my love. Kiss me with the kisses of Thy mouth. How lovely art Thou, Thy embrace. My Lord!" He spreads his arms open wide and laughs: "My lord! My love! My sole salvation! Take me to Thy lap!" He dies with his arms outstretched and a streak of blood down his chin.

Briefel explores the significance of the apple:

The apple's quasi-biblical associations are obvious as Thomasin takes on the role of temptress in relation to her brother—a few moments before, he had been uneasily eyeing her cleavage. But she herself is being seduced by her desire for the lost fruit, aligning herself explicitly and lasciviously. . . . In this case, Caleb vomits out both his mother's and his sister's desires, perhaps as punishment for the fact that he implanted them in the first place by triggering their nostalgia. (14–15)

The contrast between the agony of his body's suffering and the ecstasy of his prayer represents Christian thought on the soul's progression from the earthly, sinful body to the redeemed body. In expelling the apple from his body, he casts out the sin of sexual fantasy and seduction to beg forgiveness from God.

THE BIRTH OF A WITCH

The film makes it clear that Thomasin is expected to act as an extension of her mother in the home. This includes being physically situated in the domestic. Caleb is allowed into the woods with their father, and the twins, Mercy and Jonas, play openly about the farm. Thomasin is the only one who notices their mischief as they chant "Black Philip, we are your servants" and run freely with the goat. Thomasin tells her parents that the twins "pay her no mind," a choice of words that reveals their disrespect: she is of no importance to them. Mercy outright tells her sister, "Mother hates you." Thomasin attempts to scold them and is reprimanded for it by her parents, limiting her domestic role to a servile one.

The only time she is allowed to stray from the homestead is in this functionality, such as fetching water and washing clothes. Katherine directs her daughter to wash her father's clothes in commanding her to "Help him!" The command shows Katherine's control of her daughter as well as implicitly questioning Thomasin's value to the family. Thomasin references her servitude in telling Mercy and Jonas, "I am washing father's clothes like a slave, and thou art idle." Mercy proudly admits, "Black Philip says I can do what I like."

Distanced from the family farm and, in fact, closer to the woods, Thomasin expresses authority and possibly possession:

I will take your Black Philip. . . . It was a witch, Mercy [who stole Samuel].
You speak a-right. It was I. 'Twas I that stole him. I be the witch of the wood.
. . . I am that very witch. When I sleep, my spirit slips away from my body and
dances naked with the devil. It's there I signed his book. He bade me bring an
unbaptized babe, so I stole Sam, and I gave him to my master. And I'll make
any man or anything else vanish if I like. . . . And I'll venge thee, too, if thou
displeases me. . . . Perchance I'll boil and bake thee for lack of food. . . . How
I crave to sink my teeth into thou pink flesh!

It is Caleb who breaks her chants, an appropriate choice given his role as a
supplemental patriarchal figure. In saying that she will "take" Black Phillip,
Thomasin embraces witchcraft. Although she is not yet a witch of the woods,
her words reveal the seduction of witchcraft, with its promise of empowerment and freedom. As a witch, she would have the power to make those
who challenge and limit her to disappear and to no longer be hungry. Her
dialogue further questions her involvement in witchcraft in her warning to
Mercy that "Thou wonst tell thy mother of this! I'll witch thy mother!" After
Mercy tells her parents of Thomasin's confession near the woods, Katherine
does actually become witched.

Her words are cause for alarm because of her deviation from the ideal
woman image in showing an inverse of faith and disrupting the silent, submissive feminine model. Mary Beth Norton, author of *In the Devil's Snare:
The Salem Witchcraft Crisis of 1692*, summarizes the historical concern for
outspoken women in exploring the 1692 Salem witchcraft trials:

> Women, especially young women, were not expected to speak unbidden in
> either court or church—indeed, in the latter, they were often not expected to
> speak at all. By their intrusions into the normal ordering of Sunday services
> as well as by their disruptions in the makeshift courtroom, they signaled that
> reversals in Village life during the witchcraft crisis would not remain confined
> to individual households, but would expand to public spaces as well. (55)

Women's voices were not supposed to be heard in the private space of the
domestic nor in the public space of the church or courtroom because a
woman's voice carried newfound power and danger to the Puritan patriarchy.[3]
The concern for women was rooted in the Puritan faith since, as Schiff
notes: "Ministers . . . tended closely to female piety. They had compelling

reason to do so: the majority of every congregation was female" (144).[4] Karlsen's acknowledgement that "the work of *converting* women to subjection—and men to enlightened rule—was a central Puritan concern" corresponds to Schiff's finding and further illuminates the gendered system of power imbued within the Puritan religion (166, emphasis original). Karlsen builds upon her point, expressing: "From the beginning the message was clear: women who failed to serve men failed to serve God. To be numbered among God's elect, women had to acknowledge this service as their calling and *believe* they were created for this purpose," a statement that reveals women's subservience to men as a motivating force behind the religious paradigm (166, emphasis original). Witchcraft, then, with the image of a woman with power to disrupt order, became an issue to be taken seriously.

Thomasin's later words to her father similarly resound as an expression of power. After Caleb's death, William takes Thomasin outside into the field to question her in an attempt to obtain a confession of witchcraft. He tells her, "The bargain thou hast made has no effect . . . thy soul belongst to Christ." In doing so, he already convicts her of the crime. Her answer, however, shows her unwillingness to be silent:

> I made no bargain. . . . You ask me to speak truth? You and mother had planned to rid the farm of me. Aye, I heard you speak of it. Is that truth? You took of mother's cup and [blamed it on her] . . . confess not till it was too late. Is that truth? You are a hypocrite! You took Caleb to the wood and let me take the blame for that too. Is that truth? You let mother be as thy master. You cannot bring the crops to yield! . . . Thou cannotst do nothing save thou would!

What she says is true: William stole Katherine's prized silver cup to sell for supplies and let Katherine blame Thomasin for its disappearance. He also broke the family rule of entering the woods and did so with Caleb. Through his inability to fully assume his role as head of the household, Katherine controlled him and the family. In openly speaking her mind and defending herself, it is seen as further evidence of witchcraft. William exclaims, "Whyst I hear the devil wag thy tongue in thy mouth?" And when Thomasin accuses Mercy and Jonas of forming a covenant with the devil in the shape of Black Phillip, William further says, "Slander thy brethren no more."

William evolves from a father looking out for his family's best interests into that of a preacher and governor holding religious and secular authority

over his family. Suspecting his children of witchcraft, he refers to them in
dehumanizing terms, such as "creature," "black minions," and "grave pretend-
ers." He vows to "smite Jonas as Abraham would have done his seed" and
transforms the barn into a prison to hold his suspected children. Rather
than care for and tend to his grieving wife, who has now lost two children to
supernatural forces, he chops wood, adding to the ever-growing pile. Much
like George in *The Amityville Horror*, the father's fascination with supply-
ing firewood changes from an initial desire to enact the provider role to an
obsession with control in the face of challenging familial instability. It is the
last-ditch effort to "conquer the wilderness" that William so sought to do at
the beginning by wielding an axe to cut down the wilderness.

Following Thomasin's outburst, William resumes control of the family
and, in doing so, exerts his masculine authority. He demands that Katherine
look at their daughter and forces Thomasin to confess her accusations
against Jonas and Mercy. He imprisons Thomasin and the twins in the barn
with the goats, including Black Philip, and boards up the structure so that
they cannot escape. Once again, however, his actions lead to his family's
damnation as the witch descends upon the barn and kills the goats inside,
except for Black Philip. In a moment of self-realization, he chops wood in
an effort to provide for his family. He cries: "This is my fault. I confess it. I
confess it. Oh my God, I am at fault. I am infected with the filth of pride. I
know it. Dispose of me how Thou wilt but redeem my children. They cannot tame their natural evil. I lie before Thee a coward. . . . I beg Thee, save
my children! I beg Thee! I have damned my family!" His children were his
responsibility, however, and in failing to provide for them materially and
spiritually, he destroys his family.

He confesses to the root cause of his family's situation: by choosing his
pride over the stability of the plantation, he opens his family to the influences of the wilderness and thus witchcraft. The death of the father marks
the departure from patriarchy. He challenges Black Phillip by grabbing the
axe and exclaiming, "Corruption, thou are they father!" Black Philip rams
William in the stomach and pierces his side. His death has religious overtones
as his face, hair, and blood appear similar to Jesus on the cross.

William's arc aligns with the historical treatment of unruly women
and witches. A proper woman supported the family structure, with the
man as the head of the household; however, a deviant woman disrupted
that nuclear structure, and a witch threatened the family paradigm of

power. The family was thought of "as both 'a little Church' and 'a little Commonwealth,'" which "served as a model of relationships between God and his creatures and as model for all social relations" (Karlsen 163). A dysfunctional or fragmented family could then be seen as a handicap to the larger religious and societal structure. Individuals from such families and individuals who likewise lost their families due to various circumstances could be viewed as minorities forced to assume inferior roles, such as servants, as in the case of Mary Warren (among others) who lost her family on the Maine frontier.[5] A void in the family was particularly significant if there was no patriarch since:

> As husband, father, and master to wife, children, and servants, the head of the household stood in the same relationship to them as the minister did to his congregants and as the magistrate did to his subjects. . . . Indeed, the authority of God was vested in him as household head, and his relationship to God was immediate: he served God directly. . . . Other household members had immortal souls and could pray to God directly, but they served God indirectly by serving their superiors within the domestic frame. (Karlsen 163–64)

The relationship was clear: the men served God; in turn, the other members were expected to serve him in order to serve God. In killing all the men in the family, the witch severs that connection to the Almighty and paves the way for Thomasin's full transformation.

The fatal wound in the father's side has procreative connections reminiscent to that of Eve created from Adam's rib. From his pride and death, Thomasin completes her transformation into a witch. Just as William faces the unholy father and loses his battle for control of his family, so too does Katherine confront Thomasin. As Katherine and Thomasin fight, both of their hair becomes loose, revealing their raw emotions. Katherine even specifically grabs Thomasin by her hair, and the following dialogue ensues:

> THOMASIN: I did nothing! She came from the sky!
> KATHERINE: Devil! You have their [Jonas's and Mercy's] blood upon thy hands! It is you! It is you! . . . The devil is in thee! . . . You wreak of evil! You have made a covenant. . . . You witched thy brother! . . . You took them from me! They are gone! You killed my children! You killed thy father! You witch!

Thomasin reaches for her mother, shouting, "I'm your daughter!" Katherine recoils. Katherine tries to kill her daughter but is instead killed herself: Thomasin grabs the scythe and kills her mother by thrusting it into her mother's head. Katherine's blood is on her daughter's face as Katherine tries to choke her. The audience sees the bloodied blonde hair of Katherine as Thomasin holds her, and blood splatters around Thomasin's mouth. The murder weapon, the scythe, is a tool linked to farming and death. In using it against her mother, Thomasin severs the remaining tie to her family and life on the farm as Katherine's blood baptizes her daughter's rebirth into a witch.

FREEDOM AND LIMITATIONS

The contrast between the homestead and the dark, tree-lined woods can be interpreted as the struggle of power between the home and witchcraft, a force that allowed women to be freed from patriarchal structure of society. The untamed woods, therefore, can be read as an unruly woman, untamed by man; the very presence of it evokes fear and suspicion. It is not surprising, then, that the imagery associated with the woods in the film undermines the father's authority. We first see the woods with the witch's cottage after the witch brought back the kidnapped babe to sacrifice and renew herself. The second time is when Caleb and his father enter the woods toting a long shotgun, erect against his side, the image representing the attempt to control and exert power on the wilderness. He may not remember much of their life back in England and hold the same nostalgia for it as Thomasin does, but he is drawn to the woods for the promise of food and later sexual fulfillment. Thomasin, too, shows an attraction to the woods. She increasingly moves closer to the woods throughout the film: first when watching her baby brother and the woods in the foreground, then when washing her father's clothes in the stream, again when she and Caleb go to search for food so that she is not sent away, and finally, when she is led by the devil in the humanized form of Black Phillip.

The final moments of the movie play out as a ritual. Thomasin looks to the woods and enters the house. There, she undoes her outer dress, and the camera highlights her plump red lips, heightening the link between her sexuality and sinfulness. She holds a candle while Black Philip leads her into the barn. She speaks: "Black Philip, I conjure thee. Speak as thou didst speak to Jonas and Mercy. Dost thou understand my English tongue? Answer me."

Thomasin awaits Black Philip's offer of freedom from the Puritan patriarchy by accepting her role as a witch. © A24studio.

Her words are commanding and spoken with authority. Black Philip asks her a series of questions, including "What dost thou want?" and "Wouldst thou like to see the world?" She counters these questions, asking, "What cans thou give?" and "What will you from me?" Her counterquestions further her authority through framing the conversation as a transaction. She definitively answers, "Yes," when he asks, "Would thoust like the taste of butter? A pretty dress? Would thoust like to live deliciously?" His questions invoke sensuality and offer her a life in which she would be able to consume materials she was previously denied access to. Guided by his hand, she signs her name in his book and walks naked into the woods. Black Philip leads her to a circle of naked, chanting witches twitching on the ground, all while smeared in blood. This image is parallel to the one from the family's first night in the woods at the start of the film, including the sharp music in the background. The witches levitate around Thomasin, and as Thomasin laughs, she, too, levitates into the air smiling at her newfound freedom.

The ending questions to what extent Thomasin is free, however. In leaving her family, she breaks Christian religion. Yet to do so, she signs herself to another masculine master: the devil. In this sense, the film has no resolution. The family is beyond disrupted; they are destroyed. This marks a distinct shift from the horror films previously discussed in which the families were disassembled but ultimately came back together in the end. Instead, we now see a family whose fractures break them, allowing for the possession to fully take over their lives.

CHAPTER 8

Matrilineal Legacy
Hereditary

Hereditary is about generational horror involving a grandmother and her descendants, including her daughter and granddaughter. The film opens with the death of Ellen Leigh who, the obituary reads, passed away at her daughter Annie's home. With this, the audience is aware that Ellen and Annie's lives are intertwined from before the supernatural events began. Ellen's decisions come to define and control Annie's and her family's destinies as they all succumb to the matriarch's plan to summon and serve the demon Paimon. Annie, her husband, Steve (Gabriel Byrne), their son, Peter (Alex Wolff), and daughter, Charlie (Milly Shapiro), become unknowing participants in the true family legacy to serve the demonic.

Replicas are used throughout the film to explore moments that shape Annie. Annie works on replica miniatures for an upcoming art exhibit titled "Small World." These individual dioramas are shaped as if to fit inside of a larger house, and the subjects all relate to the domestic, including "Toiling away at Hospice" and "That and Preschool" (the titles of her works of art). Her work represents sources of power for Annie as she controls the perspective of these scenes and what happens in them. Prior to her full possession, Annie smashes the exhibit and, as a result, her identity, and she becomes an open vessel for her mother to take control of. Caetlin Benson-Allot echoes this, saying: "*Hereditary* begins with a matrilineal genealogy of trauma, as Annie (Toni Collette) recounts her painful childhood and fraught relationship with her recently deceased mother. Annie is constantly fighting for control over her life through her art (autobiographical dollhouse dioramas) and remains emotionally distant from her children, including her daughter, Charlie (Milly Shapiro)" (72). Even before the audience is introduced to any of the characters, the film plays with point of view as the viewer enters what appears to be an art studio.[1] A large file cabinet lines the wall, and the camera focuses on a miniature replica of a house with an exposed side to reveal different rooms, creating a dollhouse effect. The static, inanimate figures inside are, in fact, the family members. The camera settles on a bedroom, where a boy sleeps, and shifts to a live-action scene involving the family getting ready to attend Ellen's funeral. This start to the film thrusts the audience immediately into a sort of ongoing play with the family. The interplay between inaction and action reflects this, with the characters only coming to life once something connected with Ellen inspires them to come alive, showing that she is not just the one in control but also the one who gives the family meaning.

Jasmine Crittenden comments on the significance of the film's opening in stating, "By opening the film not just in a house, but in a house within a house, Aster extends and complicates these 'spaces of our unconscious,' creating architectural layers that are impossible to track and marking no definite points of reference" (24). It is important to note, though, that the home in which the family resides is not particularly distinct. Instead, it is a rather ordinary home, whose mundane quality adds to the horror of the film in introducing the idea that the home could belong to anyone, and by extension, the events of "grief, anger, fear, mental illness and family breakdown" that happen therein "are not exceptions to the rule, but can strike at any time" (Crittenden 25). By providing this introduction to Annie's house and domestic life, the film provides metacommentary on the domestic through establishing the connections between the exterior and interior selves.

In playing with this sense of intimacy from the beginning, the audience is invited to adopt the viewpoint of the invisible, omniscient observer. We are forced to invade the space, likening this invasion to that of Annie's mother into Annie's home. Before we are invited into this scene, however, the camera first looks outward to a nearby tree house. The interior of the tree house is illuminated and surrounded by black, lending a replica quality to the image. This introduction acts to question reality and perspective, to question whether the events that are about to unfold actually happened to the family or were created to be part of something larger and by whom. The ending of the film may provide some insight into these questions, with Paimon's followers gathered in the tree house worshipping their newly resurrected god.

FAMILY TRAUMA

The inability to take control of one's own life and family is exceptionally frustrating and terrifying for any mother. Part of the horror of *Hereditary* is Annie's attempts to separate her and her family from her mother. Annie is aware of her mother's control as well her own part in enabling it. Annie struggles to address that toxic relationship and the memories associated with it, especially once her mother dies. We see her navigating the challenging emotional landscape after Ellen dies that she was unable to during her mother's life.

Michael Koresky provides insight into this, writing: "As a depiction of family, and the particular traumas found therein, *Hereditary* plumbs some of its own nasty depths. It's an entirely discomfiting portrait of dysfunction, in which the mysterious past, chaotic present, and uncertain future of one domestic clan are in constant, fractured dialogue" (42). Attempting to probe that past to examine the present, Annie joins a grief support group, where she opens up about the underlying issues with her family:

My mom died a week ago. . . . My mom was old, and she wasn't altogether there at the end. And we were pretty much estranged before that, so it really wasn't a huge blow, but I did love her. And she didn't have an easy life. She had BiD [bipolar disorder], which became extreme at the end. And dementia. And my father died when I was a baby from starvation because he had psychotic depression and he starved himself, which I'm sure is just as pleasant as it sounds. And then there's my brother. My older brother had schizophrenia, and when he was sixteen, he hanged himself in my mother's bedroom, and, of course, his suicide note accusing her of putting people inside him, so that was my mom's life. And then she lived in our house in the end before hospice. We weren't even talking before that. We were and we weren't, and then we were. Just completely manipulative. Until my husband finally enforced a no-contact rule, which lasted until I got pregnant with my daughter. I didn't let her anywhere near me when I had my first, my son, which is why I gave her my daughter, who she immediately stabbed her hooks into.

Her speech begins with an outline of facts regarding both her mother's health and the relationship between Annie and her mother. Her repetition of the word "and" conveys that her speech is more of a litany of repressed memories that fails to process the underlying trauma. Through this conversation, the true nature of Annie's grief is revealed: loss of normalcy in her life. Annie's comment "so that's my mom's life" is passive sympathy. Although she acknowledges that her mother was "completely manipulative," resulting in Annie's husband enforcing a no-contact rule, the events in Annie's narration show her underlying guilt and obligation toward her mother while desiring to be free of her mother's influence. This influence is heavily associated with Annie's own pregnancy and motherhood: she symbolically "gave" her daughter, Charlie, to her mother out of guilt, therefore giving up her own influence over her child to please her mother. That her mother "stabbed her hooks into" Charlie reflects the sacrificial significance of that choice, when Annie's feelings of obligation toward her mother overran her maternal connection to her daughter. It is clear that legacy in the family is serving Ellen rather than the individual self. Her concluding lines show that she fears her own life, independent of her mother, will be ruined.

She delivers this confession to a circle of fellow grievers. She sits at what appears to be the head of the group. Her presence here appears coven-like and her words, commanding. Her monologue ends with "And I just . . . I felt guilty when she got sick. I just don't want to put any more stress on my family. I'm not even sure if they could give me that support. . . . Sometimes I feel like it's all ruined. And then I realize that I am to blame. Not that I'm to blame, that I am blamed." This statement opens up the discussion back to the group. The camera shows the shift in the emotions in this scene as it "mirrors the growing momentum of her dialogue, starting with a high-angle long shot that includes the group arranged in a circle around her, emphasizing her vulnerability, before it gradually zooms in on her face" (Crittenden 25). Crittenden concludes that this effect is to illicit sympathy from the viewer; however, it also serves to spotlight Annie's mental and emotional instability. The film does not share others' stories of grief from the group. That Annie's story is the only one we are privy to both shows that her story can be anyone's story as well as acts to question the relationship with her husband and children. The different houses throughout the film—in the entranceway of the family home, the tree house, and the dollhouse—can therefore be seen as reminders that, at any given moment, the audience is only ever viewing one of a multitude of realities and stories.

Annie's eulogy provides insight into the tumultuous relationship with her mother. She wears a pendant that matches the one her mother wore as she delivers this eulogy, implying the cycle of life and death and a postmortem obligation to her mother. Annie describes her mother as a "very secretive and private woman," implying that her mother was closed off even to her own daughter, with her "private rituals, private friends, private anxieties." She continues:

> It honestly feels like a betrayal just to be standing here talking about her. She was a very difficult woman to read. If you ever thought you knew what was going on with her, and God forbid you try to confront that. . . . But when her life was unpolluted, she could be the sweetest, warmest, loving person in the world. She was also incredibly stubborn, which maybe explains me. You could always count on her to always have the answer. And if she ever was mistaken, that was your opinion, and you were wrong.

The words present Ellen as a controlling figure, directing others' actions and lives. The structure of Annie's sentences reveals her conflicting feelings toward her mother. Ellen was both nurturing and tainted, indicating the maternal dichotomy of the good mother and deviant mother. Ellen is also characterized as a matriarch and as the family member others turned to for answers; these answers were final and not open to debate. She could be both intimate and distant in her affection. This scene is interplayed with ones from the wake in which strangers rub and bless the lifeless lips of the deceased, paying ritualistic homage to her, raising the question of who else could be considered Ellen's family. It heightens Ellen's status to that of a god, with a flock that continues to worship and pay homage to her.

ELLEN'S MATRIARCHY

At home, Annie works on her upcoming art exhibit "Small World," a series of miniature replica houses that contain intimate scenes from her life. This art installation becomes Annie's coping mechanism for both her mother's death and the later death of her daughter, Charlie. Through creating this art, Annie expresses controlled reflection over sites of trauma.

One such scene features a figure of her dying mother in a hospital bed. The figure Annie works on is that of the doctor, signaling that her own character is one who hopes to heal and be a caretaker. Later, she tucks in her daughter, Charlie, and addresses the death of Charlie's grandmother:

> ANNIE: You know you were her favorite, right? Even when you were a little baby, she wouldn't let me feed you because she needed to feed you.
>
> CHARLIE: She wanted me to be a boy.
>
> ANNIE: You know, I was a tomboy when I was growing up. I hated dresses and dolls and pink.
>
> CHARLIE: Who's going to take care of me?
>
> ANNIE: Um, excuse me, you don't think I'm not going to take care of you?
>
> CHARLIE: But when you die?
>
> ANNIE: Then Dad will take care of you. And Peter. . . . You never cried as a baby. Even when you were born.

The repetition of "you know" is meant to remind Charlie of her relationship to her grandmother as well as to highlight Annie's feelings of resentment toward her mother. Charlie occupied a place Annie hoped to aspire to: that of Ellen's favorite. Annie compares herself to her daughter growing up in her memory of her as a "tomboy," a nickname for a girl who does not embody traditionally feminine characteristics. Annie's language highlights the tenuous relationship she had with her mother, citing how Ellen, not Charlie's own mother, fed Charlie as a baby. This omen hints at a supernatural link between Charlie and Ellen, one that is made more present by the word "Satony" scribbled on Charlie's wall; "Satony" is a word that closely resembles "Satan." In Ellen feeding Charlie as a baby, she imprints herself and her occult agenda on her granddaughter from a young age by taking away a pivotal bonding moment between mother and child.

Ellen's reproductive agency transforms her into the archaic mother. As Creed explains: "The central characteristic of the archaic mother is her total dedication to the generative, procreative principle. She is the mother who conceives all by herself, the original parent, the godhead of all fertility and the origin of procreation. She is outside morality and the law" (27). In creating her art and recreating her life, Annie wears magnifiers that intensify the

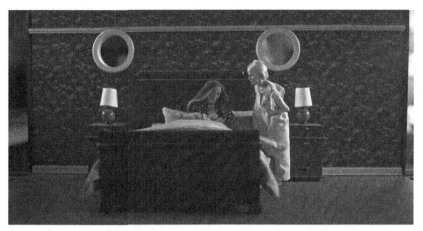

Annie recreates her mother breastfeeding Charlie as a baby. © A24studio.

details and reflect the scrutiny with which she examines moments of her life. She purposely chooses to recreate the scene of Charlie's first feeding from Ellen's breast to explore her mother's progenitive power. The miniature figure of Ellen is clearly aged and elderly yet is able to produce milk for the infant Charlie, while Annie lays bedridden. The holes in the back of the diorama connect with the two circular mirrors behind Annie's bed, both similar to a set of eyes watching the characters.

This becomes clear as Annie goes through her mother's belongings, specifically a box titled "Mom's things," a label that speaks to the compartmentalization of her relationship with her mother. In this box is a book called *Notes on Spiritualism*, along with a note her mother left her, reading:

My darling, dear, beautiful Annie,
    Forgive me all the things I could not tell you. Please don't hate me and try not to despair your losses. You will see in the end that they were worth it.
    Our sacrifice will pale next to the rewards.
    Love, Mummy.

What is not said is that these losses include that of Annie's daughter, husband, herself, and her son. Ellen says "our sacrifice," linking her with her daughter. The film makes this intertwining of mother and daughter evident in the featured miniature scene containing figures representing Annie, her mother, and baby Charlie. In the miniature, Annie lays in bed as if to nurse her daughter, only it is her mother's engorged breasts that supply the breast-milk. The figures note the deeper issues of motherhood at play in the film as Ellen is cast as the maternal figurehead, while Annie assists her mother, albeit unknowingly, in Ellen's plans to groom Charlie for the demon Paimon. Ellen's choice to sign her name as "Mummy" posits the relationship she has with her adult daughter as still that of a mother and a young child. Her rhetoric likewise shows this dynamic with the phrases "forgive me" and "please don't hate me," reading more as commands.[2] The lines "you will see in the end that they were worth it" and "our sacrifice will pale next to the rewards" remind Annie that her mother is the one with executive agency in the relationship, even from beyond the grave.

FAMILY RELATIONSHIPS

Annie desires a structured, normal family life that is in opposition to the one she experienced as a child. Her desire for normalcy is seen in her relationship with Charlie. She berates her daughter for walking around outside with no coat and no shoes, asking her, "Are you some kind of idiot?" Charlie answers her mother's harsh question by saying, "I want Grandma," a response that undermines Annie's maternal relationship by expressing desire for her grandmother, her surrogate mother. Annie roughly handles her daughter on the walk to the house where she tells Charlie that she is going to a party with her brother, an ambiguous gathering she terms "some school hangout with other kids." When Charlie asks why she is being forced to go, her mother candidly informs her, "Because you get to hang out with other kids . . . with your brother, with other kids." Given the proximity of this scene with that of the grief-support-group dialogue, the film implies that perhaps Charlie's forced social interaction is a projection of Annie's own repressed feelings of guilt and loss over her older brother.

Despite their own tumultuous relationship, Annie loves her daughter very much. She is the parent who tucks Charlie into bed the night after the funeral. Charlie's bedroom is bathed in warm light and filled with various pieces of her art, multimedia creatures she creates out of found materials; she, like her mother, is an artist. Charlies asks who's going to take care of her after Annie dies, showing Annie is Charlie's primary caregiver. After discovering Charlie's decapitated body in her car, Annie screams on the floor of her bedroom in

Steve (Gabriel Byrne) holds Annie as she grieves their daughter's death. © A24studio.

grief while her husband holds her. Her back-and-forth motion mimic that of both an animal giving birth as well as a woman grieving; these parallels symbolize the birthing of the supernatural events to come as well as a release of Annie's emotions. She cries: "I can't! I can't! I just wanna die. . . . It hurts too much!" She sleeps outside in the tree house, where Charlie would often sleep, enrobed in the red light from the heater. The tree house, distanced from the construct of the main house, stands among the white oak trees that support, surround, and mark it as a space aligned with the wilderness. In sleeping in the tree house, Charlie and Annie show a desire to return to the primal mother, with the heater transforming the space into a symbolic womb or incubator. It is in this location that the movie ends as Charlie finds rebirth in Peter's body, their true identity of Paimon realized.

Although her husband is a doctor and physically present for Annie, he remains largely unsupportive of her and fails to help her process her pain. She asks permission from Steve to sleep in the tree house to mourn Charlie. She recreates the scene of the accident in miniature form, including Charlie's decapitation. She calls it a "neutral view of the accident," phrasing that demonstrates her attempt to process the trauma from it. When Steve sees this, his immediate concern is for their son and how Peter will feel when he sees it. It is clear that Steve is more concerned with his son's feelings than his wife's and echoes this in telling her "Come, stay, I don't give a shit" in regard to her eating dinner that night. He asks Annie, "What's our deadline?" And he asks whether she has thought about titles for her upcoming art exhibit,

Annie's moment of emotional catharsis at the dinner table. © A24studio.

undermining Annie's creative authority in overseeing her work. All of Annie's work is his work, her emotions ones that he regulates and controls.

Steve's prioritization of Peter over Annie becomes clear at the dinner table that night. Annie and Peter engage in a heated conversation. Peter inquires about his mother's well-being, asking, "Is there something on your mind?" Annie mimics the question to Peter, and he comments that there appears to be something she wants to say. She opens up:

> ANNIE: I mean, why would I want to say something, so I can watch you sneer at me? . . . I don't want to say anything.
> PETER: Just say it! Just fucking say it!
> ANNIE: Don't you swear at me, you little shit! Don't you ever raise your voice at me! . . . Well, now your sister is dead! And I know you miss her, and I know it was an accident, and I know you're in pain, and I wish I could take that away for you. I wish I could shield you from the knowledge that you did what you did. . . . But you can't take responsibility for anything! So, now I can't accept, and I can't forgive! Because nobody admits anything they've done!

Annie sits back down to her plate, a move that is in stark contrast to her emotional catharsis. Koresky notes potential meaning behind this, saying: "Annie shuttles from indifference to desperation, self-awareness to oblivious-ness, pragmatism to insanity. Gradually we begin to wonder how much of this behavior is really Annie, and how much can be attributed to something that's perhaps taken control of her" (44). Peter stares at her and, true to Annie's prediction, sneers at her, saying: "What about you, Mom? She didn't want to go to the party. So why was she there?" In doing so, Peter attempts to project his guilt and responsibility for his sister's death onto his mother as well as undermine her authority. That Charlie's death happened in Annie's car, while Peter was driving, furthers this by positing Peter as an active agent who deepens the instability of the family. An agent of Charlie's death, he chooses to leave her decapitated corpse to rot in their mother's car and, presumably, for Annie to take care of without thought to her emotions.

Joan (Ann Dowd), a woman from the grief group, asks Annie to describe her relationship with her son. She responds, saying that she suffers from sleepwalking but has not done so in years because the last time she did, she almost killed her son. She stood next to Peter with a can of paint thinner and a box of matches. She recalls:

> And I woke myself up striking a match, which also woke Peter up, and he was screaming. And I immediately put the match out. I mean, I was just as shocked as he was. And it was impossible to convince them it was just sleep-walking, which it was. But the timing was awful. Peter and I had gotten into this stupid quarreling phase, forever arguing about nothing. Such frivolous stuff. And Peter always held it against me. And there's nothing I can say, and there's nothing I can do because it happened. While I was asleep.

Her continued use of "and" in recalling the memory structures her sentences in a way that objectively lists the actions that took place during the experience. She refers to the rest of her family as "them," positing herself as an outsider in the domestic. The blame and guilt she feels and which her family places on her depicts her as a neglectful, abusive mother so unaware that it put her child in danger. In reality, however, it is much more complicated. She was forced into motherhood by her mother, and her son serves as both a constant reminder of that and adds to the masculine control over her.

Annie's description of Charlie's death as a "waste" because it serves no purpose for the family shows the family as fractured even before her death. Annie's response exposes her true feelings and the emotional labor that is invisible to her son and husband. She exclaims: "I am your mother. . . . All I do is worry and slave and defend you." She adds, "all I get back is that fucking face . . . so full of disdain and resentment and always so annoyed," words that stress the undervaluing of her maternal role in the household. Peter's face can also be read as an extension of Steve's face, marking the domineering homelife Annie lives in and seeks to escape from in her art. Her speech holds Peter accountable for Charlie's death in exposing his lack of responsibility, stymieing Annie's recovery from the trauma as well as showing the contrast in the treatment of women and men in the home: women suffer at men's passivity. Steve is the one to end this conversation and Annie's emotional catharsis. She walks away from the table, leaving the two men to continue eating. Steve extends a hand to his son, leaving his wife unsupported and defenseless.

CHARLIE'S DEATH AND REBIRTH

Charlie's death serves to destabilize Annie's mental and emotional state. She reaches out to Joan, seeking support. Joan, however, is revealed to be an agent of Annie's mother and uses Annie's vulnerability to accelerate Peter's possession. Joan shows Annie how to conduct a séance to contact the dead, even providing Annie with a handout supposedly from a psychic medium. She tells Annie that every member in the house needs to be home to perform the phenomenon to link all the family members together. From this experiment, Annie wakes up Steve and Peter to declare that she is, in fact, a medium. While performing the ceremony, Charlie draws in her notebook, a glass moves across the table, and the flame rises from the candle. The presence of Charlie's notebook is of particular importance because she would recreate scenes in it. Like her mother, she would use her art to understand and process reality. Now deceased, she relies on it as a means of communication.

Peter begins crying in his father's arms, a regressive gesture that posits Peter as in boyhood. At school, Peter begins to see visions of a light orb, and his reflection takes on an agency of its own. Steve calls Annie about the incident, saying: "Peter just called me in hysterics from the hallway. Thinks he's being threatened by some vengeful spirit. . . . Listen to me, Annie, I have a son to protect. . . . That's what I'm worried about right now." Steve's choice of words again undermines Peter's masculinity, describing him as being in "hysterics," a word with roots in "hysteria," a once-believed medical condition that was used to dismiss women's mental health concerns and issues.

His words also show a lack of support for Annie's grief, instead prioritizing his son's mental health over that of his wife's. Annie defends herself, telling him that Peter is "[her] son, too." This conversation takes place while Annie is in her workshop working on her installment. The piece she works on is the interior of the funeral home the day she gave her mother's eulogy. The gallery calls, leaving her a voicemail to check in on her and to say that they are willing to "help in any way." Annie smashes her workshop in response, preserving the decapitated figure of Charlie's head in her bed.

Peter's role in the film is very much that of a passive stoner until the supernatural begins. Often seen smoking a bong, he is portrayed as associated with toxic masculinity. He feels nothing over the death of his grandmother, a shared ambivalence he and his father bond over. He stares fixated on a classmate's posterior during class, ignoring the teacher and the discussion around him. He receives a text message from his friend, who invites him to a party and tells him to "bring your dick!" Once at that party, he abandons his little sister to go upstairs to smoke. When Charlie begins to go into anaphylactic shock, having eaten a chocolate cake with nuts—the very food she is allergic to—Peter chooses to drive her to the hospital in an attempt to both save his little sister and himself from enduring trouble. The language and Peter's actions reveal him to be a toxic male character, one whose decisions are motivated by phallic-centered desires and selfishness. She opens the window in the backseat to try to get fresh air, and in swerving to avoid a dead animal in the road and a light post, Peter decapitates her. He does not retrieve her head; in doing so, he kills her just as he would an animal on the road. He slowly drives away and returns back home, where he lays down in his bedroom, leaving Charlie's decapitated body in the backseat of his parents' car.[3] Annie is the one to discover the horror, and her screams fill the background of the scene. Peter's lack of action and voice are notable throughout this; even at his sister's funeral, as they lower her casket into the ground, Peter looks on indifferently while Annie is wailing. He is shown as a naturally destructive and chaotic character, and the women in his family are the ones to suffer for it.

This indifferent expression as well as lack of voice and agency establish an almost trancelike quality to Peter's existence, one that foreshadows his possession. At lunch, he sits by himself and hears Joan calling his voice from across the street, chanting: "I expel you! . . . Peter, get out!" Joan's chant is meant to remove Peter from his body, thus rendering his existence to be no more than a vessel for Paimon, the god of mischief. Annie reads a description of Paimon in a book:

> When successfully invoked, King Paimon will possess the *vulnerable* host. Only when the ritual is *complete* will King Paimon be locked into his ordained host. Once locked in, a new ritual is required to *unlock* the possession. . . . The sexes of the hosts have varied, but the most successful incarnations have been with men, and it is documented that King Paimon has become livid and vengeful when offered a female host. For these reasons, it is imperative to remember that King Paimon is male, thus covetous of a male human body.

Charlie was the initial host of Paimon. Like in the paragraph's description of Paimon, she was vengeful unto herself in that her death came at the hands of chocolate cake, which she did not ask the ingredients of. When a pigeon flies against the window of her classroom, she decapitates it and attaches it to an empty pill container. Once Charlie is deceased, Paimon's followers seek to put Charlie, and therefore Paimon, into Peter's body, similar to Charlie's earlier creation.

Realizing what is happening to her family, Annie makes a last-minute attempt to save her son. She warns Steve: "They put a curse on us when we brought Charlie back. We made a pact with something. Something that is in this house." She blames herself for the danger her family is in, saying: "I'm sorry, Steve, I'm don't know what I did, but Peter is in danger, and I started it. If you destroy this book, it will take me too. . . . I am linked to it. If we don't destroy it, Peter will. . . . We have to do it. Please, please, for Peter." Her guilt over what is happening to her family is a maternal one. She feels she has unleashed this power onto her family, and she must be the one to end it, even if it means taking her own life. She birthed it, and now she must destroy it. She has a can of paint thinner ready to burn the sketchbook. Both items are linked to her identity as an artist and, symbolically, through her maternity, with paint thinner representing amniotic fluid. In burning the sketchbook and presumably ending her own life, the paint thinner becomes a destructive symbol of maternity. Paint thinner is tied to the act of erasing; its role in the film subverts the symbolic amniotic fluid to show an inverse creation. Annie uses the paint thinner to try to kill her son, and it is used to kill her husband. She evolves into the maternal figure of both creator and destroyer in order to allow her mother, in turn, to ascend to these dual roles as well.

Annie watches, trancelike, as her husband burns. No longer marred by her controlling husband, her destiny as a performer in the spectacle of possession begins as she herself becomes possessed in the ritual. Her possessed state corresponds to her repressed emotions. She charges at Peter, who pleads: "Mom, please stop! I'm sorry! Mommy, please, I'm begging you to stop." He refers to her in an infantile tone, regressing to an earlier stage to appeal to her motherhood. He hides in the attic where, unbeknownst to him, the pinnacle of the ritual is about to take place. There are lit candles, a circle in the corner, an outline of a body in ash with a candle near the groin area. He looks up and sees Annie levitating and sawing her head off with piano wire. Towering above him in the air, her self-induced decapitation symbolizes her break with patriarchal control and influence. Peter jumps out the window and lands face-first into the garden. The spectacle of her decapitation forces Peter to confront the fate he doomed Charlie to. Rather than stay and confront this scene, he chooses death.

An orb of light enters him from his back. Rising, he sees his mother's headless body levitate into the tree house, where an orange glow emanates. He sees naked coven members standing in the woods as the camera adopts his point of view walking into the tree house, where, inside, more elderly individuals are kneeling and bowing in prayer. He sees the effigy of Paimon standing in the center, an image that is Jesus-like due to its crown. In front of it are the decapitated mother and grandmother, their bodies kneeling in prayer. He turns to face the kneeling members as the camera shows a picture of Queen Leigh hanging on the wall. Joan takes the crown from the effigy and places it on Peter's head, saying:

> Oh, hey, it's alright, Charlie. You're alright now. You are Paimon, one of the ancient kings of hell. We have looked to the northwest and called you in. We've corrected your first female body and give you now this healthy, male host. We reject the Trinity and pray devoutly to you, great Paimon. Give us your knowledge of all secret things. Bring us honor, wealth, and good familiars. Bind all men to our will, as we have bound ourselves for now and ever to yours. Hail Paimon!

Charlie has been completely transformed into Paimon, inside of Peter's body. The last scene in the tree house speaks to one of the main tropes of the film: that an individual's destiny can be predestined by their family. Ellen, the grandmother—and matriarch of the film—bound herself and her lineage to the fulfillment of this ritual. When Annie gave birth to a girl and not a boy with Charlie, Ellen ensured Paimon's resurrection by literally and symbolically nursing Charlie's identity from birth. Peter, in contrast, was raised by Annie. Unbeknownst to both Annie and Peter, his passivity would render him the ideal vessel for possession.

FORCED MOTHERHOOD

The film highlights issues surrounding Annie's motherhood and her relationship with Peter. Often, these insights are seen through sleep, such as the sleepwalking incident from years ago. She envisions ants crawling over the bed and sheets just as they crawled over Charlie's decapitated head. She sees them coming in from the windowsill and walks into Peter's room, where they are covering his face and pillow. The ants show the relationship between the characters as Charlie's death will infest and consume the family.

The conversation Annie and Peter have highlights the family's ominous end. In a dream, she admits that she never wanted to be a mother, but Ellen pressured her to have children, and in doing so, Annie ensured her mother's legacy. The following conversation takes place between Annie and Peter during that dream:

> PETER: Then why did you have me?
> ANNIE: It wasn't my fault! I tried to stop it!
> PETER: How?
> ANNIE: I tried to have a miscarriage.
> PETER: How?
> ANNIE: However I could. I did everything they told me not to do, but it didn't work. I'm happy it didn't work.
> PETER: You tried to kill me!
> ANNIE: [Shaking her head] I love you! I tried to save you . . .
> PETER: [Crying] You tried to kill me!

In stating her aversion to having children and her attempts to end the pregnancy, Annie becomes an abject mother. Her attempts, trying to have a miscarriage and then trying to save Peter, contrast and show her dual maternity as creator and destroyer. The dream ends with both mother and son crying as they are each increasingly doused in paint thinner. A match is lit, and Annie becomes engulfed in flames, symbolic of penance for her sin.

Her guilt in this episode serves as the catalyst for the séance to contact Charlie. Annie wakes Peter up, apologizing: "I'm so, so sorry for everything, all the things I said." She then gets Peter up so that the three of them can conduct the séance downstairs. She urges, "We need to do this as a family." The organization of these scenes acts to highlight Annie as a deviant, destructive mother. She is depicted as a mother who is creator, destroyer, and recreator in the film. She recreates significant scenes from her and her family's life, and later she helps to recreate Charlie in the form of Paimon in Peter's body.

Peter dreams that he wakes up to the sound of Charlie popping her mouth and sees the apparition of his sister in the corner of the room. Her head moves forward and drops, but it is a ball on the floor. He sees a dog growing in the doorway, an animal associated with witches and the devil. A pair of arms grab him from the headboard, and he screams. He wakes up to Annie in the room, and Peter accuses her of being the one trying to pull his head off. She claims that she is going to stop what is happening and is the only one who can "fix this."

In trying to save her family, Annie only damns them further. She takes Charlie's sketchbook and throws it into the fire only to have her arm catch fire instead, forcing her to abandon her task. Realizing the maternal connection between the object and Charlie's spirit, she later decides to toss the sketchbook into the fire again despite the danger it presents. She says a tearful goodbye to Steve as she readies herself to be engulfed in flames while the book burns. He is the one, however, who catches on fire. The fire consumes his body until it is blackened, with only his gold wedding band remaining intact. For Steve to die, not Annie, represents the death of the father and death of the patriarchal influence. As Annie watches him die by fire, her face changes from horror to possession. The emotional shock of his family's unfolding causes Peter to weep uncontrollably. The parallel between the lack of emotion in Annie and Peter's outpouring of emotion is keeping with Clover's theory on emotional spaces in horror: "For a space to be created in which men can weep without being labeled feminine, women must be relocated to a space where they will be made to wail uncontrollably; for men to be able to relinquish emotional rigidity, control, women must be relocated to a space in which they will undergo a flamboyant psychotic break" (105). Annie stalks

Peter through the home until he hides upstairs in the attic. There, he sees his mother levitating and sawing off her own head, the third and final woman to be decapitated. First, her mother's body is found without her head, then Charlie is decapitated, and, finally, Annie is as well. The series of decapitations aligns with the family lineage from mother to daughter to granddaughter. Charlie cuts off the head of a dead pigeon and attaches it to an empty pill bottle. In the tree house, the entity of Charlie/Paimon that possesses Peter's body witnesses the decapitated bodies bowing before Paimon's effigy.

The film starts and ends with the image of a home. At the start, it is the family home the audience enters. By the end of the film, the family home has been abandoned in favor of the tree house. The tree house thus comes to stand for a wild house, one that does not abide by the patriarchal structure of the traditional home. It is a tangible extension of the wild and unknown, the blurring of the masculine and feminine.

Motherhood Revisited

I end this book by addressing the title. What does the "sinful maternal" mean? It means to deviate from that which we associate with motherhood: the qualities of being nurturing, caring, protective, compassionate, and, above all, dedication of their entire self to their children. To not fully embody these characteristics is to go against womanhood itself. Yet it's also what every woman does. The sinful maternal, then, is the reality women face every day: that in not being a good enough mother, or not even wanting motherhood, a woman has transgressed and sinned against what her role in the world is perceived to be.

"Why can't you just be normal?" It is the line Amelia shouts to Samuel as he has a tantrum in the backseat of her car in *The Babadook*. They have just been kicked out of Ruby's birthday party after Samuel pushed her out of the tree house. Still processing her son's outburst, she drives home and tries to remain calm as her son's cries increase in volume. He screams, and the piercing sound causes her calm façade to break.

The scene is so poignant in its relatability. Normalcy is the desired hope mothers have for their children. Of course, normalcy is relative and an impossible concept to truly define. The most accepted definition of normalcy in children is for nothing to be wrong with them. This idea is extremely problematic, however, since it allows for any number of issues to be ignored or dismissed.

Normalcy is also a desired goal for motherhood. To enter into motherhood is to enter into a state of the unknown. Countless fears permeate the mind, and even after a child enters the world, mothers are constantly afraid for their health and safety. While fulfilling, motherhood can be isolating, traumatizing, and downright terrifying.

Women are constantly told to become mothers and the right way to mother. We are inundated with messages from society, culture, politics, government, and religion, not to mention those we call our loved ones. We adopt these ideals others force upon us as the standards by which we judge ourselves. When we do not meet these unrealistic expectations, we nonetheless feel the sting of disappointment.

Susan Douglas and Meredith Michaels's book *The Mommy Myth: The Idealization of Motherhood and How It Has Undermined Women* examines these unrealistic and oppressive expectations. The core of the book is the concept of "new momism," which they define as:

> The insistence that no woman is truly complete or fulfilled unless she has kids, that women remain the primary caretakers of children, and that to be a remotely decent mother, a woman has to devote her entire physical, psychological, emotional, and intellectual being, 24/7, to her children. The new momism is a highly romanticized and yet demanding view of motherhood in which the standards for success are impossible to meet. (Douglas and Michaels 4)[1]

This romanticization largely applies to mothers who are in relationships. As we've seen in *The Amityville Horror*, *The Conjuring 2*, and *The Babadook*, single mothers are often ostracized and viewed as lacking because of the status of their relationships. Yet even those in relationships can feel disillusioned by expectations versus the realities of motherhood. And there are those whose decisions to become mothers were never actually theirs to make; instead, it was expected and sometimes forced on them.

Possession films act on this ever-present fear by endangering children either through direct possession or possessing the parent. If the child is possessed, the power of the parent—typically the religious or spiritual authority—must expel the possessing entity to restore order to the family. If a parent is possessed, they must remember their families and fight the possession from the inside to show that their love for their family outweighs any demonic influence.

Horror is a genre whose use of the monstrous allows it to push back against these expectations and call for more realistic narratives of motherhood. *Rosemary's Baby* depicts the terror of women not having control over their bodies and of women's reproductive health taken from them. *The Conjuring*'s Lorraine shows the struggle of a working mother being away from her daughter and the guilt of being absent from the home. Both Kathy from *The Amityville Horror* and Katherine in *The Witch* must navigate their identities as wives and mothers to protect their families from unseen forces and, in the process, rebel against repressive roles. Chris in *The Exorcist* and Renai in *Insidious* experience the plight of mothers unable to help their sick children. This is an experience Peggy in *The Conjuring 2* and Amelia from *The Babadook* also endure, and these difficulties are compounded by a lack of support from medical, political, and personal individuals.

And, of course, there is Annie's journey in *Hereditary*. Her horror began long before her mother passed. Coerced to become pregnant and forced to be a mother by her own, the Annie we see from the start is one who has long been imprisoned by continual maternal expectations. Hers is a story marked by loss as she loses everyone she held close to her in the name of resurrecting a god and completing her mother's legacy.

The films highlighted in this book are by no means an exhaustive compilation of motherhood in horror nor was that the intention when writing this.[2] I instead wanted to highlight issues of motherhood in select possession films. Anxieties surrounding motherhood are common themes in horror cinema. Alfred Hitchcock's *Psycho* (1960) is a prime example of this, with Norman Bates possessed by the memory of his mother, which drives his murderous spirit. In terms of more recent horror, Kimberly Peirce's 2013 adaptation of *Carrie* expands on the original 1976 film by including more background on Carrie's mother and her daughter's birth.[3] Another adaptation that centers more on the mother-daughter relationship is Mary Lambert's *Pet Sematary* (2019). Unlike the original film, in which the son dies and is brought back to life, this time it is the daughter who comes back from the dead.[4] Alice Lowe's horror comedy *Prevenge* (2016) is about a pregnant widow who thinks she hears her baby telling her to kill. The movie addresses issues of grief, trauma, and, similar to *Rosemary's Baby*, concerns about pregnancy and impending parenthood.[5] Emmanuel Osei-Kuffour's *Black Box* (2020) is an interesting twist on the possession narrative as a mother uses her medical knowledge and resources to transplant her dead son's consciousness into that of another patient in the hopes of resurrecting her child.

Mothers in horror films love to scream—out of fear, survival, and love. As audience members, we share these screams. We are unafraid of the monsters and horrors they face (well, maybe a little afraid). The hope is that, after the credits roll, their bravery gives us inspiration to reshape longstanding, conformist ideas of women, maternity, and motherhood into ones that grant us independence and agency.

NOTES

INTRODUCTION. IT COMES FROM INSIDE: HORROR, HOME, AND POSSESSION

1. Haunted houses have existed in horror cinema since its inception. The 1896 short film *The House of the Devil* (also known as *The Haunted Castle* or *Le Manoir du diable*) shows the devil causing mischief and fright in a castle. What is considered to be the first full-length haunted-house film is the 1927 silent movie *The Cat and the Canary*, in which a greedy family is tested and stalked by someone who, in fact, turns out to be human.

2. This transformation process almost always takes a toll on the physical body. Rosemary's body becomes skeletal and her eyes, sunken as a result of her pregnancy. She suffers intense, debilitating pain. Regan also suffers, being thrown about her bed and her body morphed to resemble the demonic. Janet's face also changes to have a more sunken expression. In the height of her possession, Janet's face takes on a bluish tinge and her eyes become inhuman.

3. Thomasin's transformation rebaptizes her as a witch and servant of the devil. The ending shows her naked and covered in her mother's blood as she accepts Black Philip's offer of a new life. This transformation is an inversion of the Christian baptism, in which holy water is applied to an individual to cleanse them of their original sin. The blood of her mother acts to re-mark Thomasin with sin.

4. This is not to say that possession films were not released during the other decades not included in the book. Possession films from the 1980s include Stanley Kubrick's *The Shining* (1980), Sam Raimi's 1981 cult classic *The Evil Dead*, and John Carpenter's *The Thing* (1982). Although *The Shining* is a film in which a mother and son are impacted by the possession of the father, Jack Torrance's possession in that movie is never made explicit. Kubrick deviated from Stephen King's original work by introducing Jack Torrance as a character who is unstable from the start, making it unclear whether his escalating actions are the result of possession or his own repressed issues. In the novel, Jack has more room for possible redemption. The relationship between Wendy and Danny Torrance is also limited in that film in favor of exploiting the different horrors the hotel contains.

CHAPTER 1. POSSESSED BY PREGNANCY: *ROSEMARY'S BABY*

1. The sweeping view of the city skyline shows the grandeur Rosemary envisions as she sings the lullaby. Rosemary is, after all, the one who tells Guy for them to take the apartment.

2. Her name is also evocative of Minnie Mouse, a cartoonish character whose purpose is to entertain. Minnie's role also to entertain in keeping Rosemary distracted and placated. Minnie wears bright colors and large jewelry and hats, lending a cartoonish characteristic to her. She also calls the chocolate mousse laced with sedative chocolate mouse, another reference to keeping Rosemary unaware of the realities around her.

3. The Castevets disguise their satanic agenda behind goodwill toward Terry. According to Terry, they took her off the streets and gave her a home. It is implied that when she found out their true intentions, she jumped to her death. Minnie's voice echoes through the apartment wall, berating Roman that she told him Terry would not be open minded. Open-mindedness is an interesting characteristic to associate with their plans to summon the antichrist, and this shows that they believe they are progressive in their beliefs.

4. With no job, no career, and no other identity than being Guy's wife, Rosemary depends on her husband for more than finances. He gives her identity and self-worth. She is rarely seen without him, and when she is, she undergoes experiences that cause her to have a heightened sense of fear.

5. Judas agreed to turn Jesus into the Romans in exchange for thirty pieces of silver. He revealed who Jesus was with a kiss. Here, Rosemary pays Guy the quarter in exchange for the knowledge that she is pregnant and the feeling that her husband genuinely cares about her and her pregnancy.

6. Rosemary cries, "It's alive!" when she first feels the baby kick. Before this, she began to have doubts about the healthiness of the pregnancy. The exuberance with which she delivers the line is eerily similar to that of Victor Frankenstein's in *Frankenstein* (1931) when he sees his creature show signs of life.

7. It is important to remember that Catholicism was not always an accepted religion. Historically, Catholics have been viewed the same way Satanists and witches were: as evil. For more information, see Aiello.

8. The normalization of Rosemary's pain during pregnancy harkens back to Eve's sin in the Garden of Eden and the punishment that women should be made to suffer, especially in regard to childbirth.

CHAPTER 2. PUBERTY AS HELL: *THE EXORCIST*

1. It is also in the basement that Chris confides in Father Karras that there is nothing he could do that would cause further harm to her daughter. The basement is thus the origin of the possession and the site of the beginning of the end of it.

2. She opens her mouth to show a bloodied inside, foreshadowing her inverse fertility.

3. *The Exorcist II: The Heretic* (1977) revisits Pazuzu's possession by revealing that the demon attacks those who, in fact, have psychic abilities that can be used to heal people. Regan's insistence on a father figure and romantic companion for her mother could be her interpreting her mother's own romantic and parental loss.

4. See S. Williams.

5. Although this line may read as a rejection of her daughter, Chris refuses to believe that her daughter is corrupted and incapable of being saved. Pazuzu's possession can not only be interpreted as an attempt to expel the invasive paternal but also the maternal presence.

6. Father Karras is another character who wrestles with his relationship with his parents. His mother ends up in a state-run mental hospital because he does not have money for a

private one. His uncle comments, "If you weren't a priest, you'd be a famous psychiatrist" and that his mother would be living in a penthouse. This conflict is representative of Karras's choice to follow his spiritual father's path and its impact on his earthly mother. As he walks to the end of the room to see her, the other patients reach out to him, showing the conflict between his public and private self.

7. The demon reminds Karras of his failure to save his mother. Because of this failing, saving Regan is his redemptive act.

8. *The Exorcist II: The Heretic* builds on this idea by showing that Regan's memories of her possession are repressed.

Chapter 3. The House Remembers: *The Amityville Horror*

1. In doing so, Kathy uses consumerism to get her aunt to stay. When Helena continues to leave, Kathy tells George to "make her stay," attempting to use patriarchal intimidation. Both read as desperate attempts to show off their newfound status of the house since, as a nun, Helena would be expected to reject materialism and would answer to a higher authority: God.

2. After waking up from a dream in which she is given insight into the DeFeo murders, she investigates what happened in the house. She takes the family van to the newspaper office and sees a photo of DeFeo and realizes he looks just like George. When she arrives home, she hides her children from her husband out of fear that history will repeat itself.

3. The eyelike windows are often shown in their height overlooking the action and characters below, suggesting that the Lutz family is constantly being watched as well as shaping the house as something alive.

4. The room that the boys play in during this scene is the same one that ejects Father Delaney and where George thinks he sees flies infesting the window. Kathy calls it her room and does not appear negatively affected by it. Because of this, the window closing on the son's hand can be read as the house again rejecting the masculine.

Chapter 4. Danger All Around: *Insidious* and *Insidious: Chapter 2*

1. The *Insidious* films extend beyond the first two films discussed in this chapter. *Insidious: Chapter 3* (2015), *Insidious: The Last Key* (2018), and *Insidious: The Red Door* (2023) also comprise the franchise. While the films share the same cosmology of the Further, they differ in terms of plot, main characters, and the family in danger, with the exception of the upcoming *Insidious: The Red Door*, which will be a sequel to *Insidious* and *Insidious: Chapter 2*. *Insidious* and *Insidious: Chapter 2* are emphasized because the plot of the first film extends into that of the second rather than featuring a new family.

2. The ability to move houses hints at the family's privilege and socioeconomic status. Similar to *The Amityville Horror*, suburbia is shown as a trap that imprisons families in a cycle of debt, repression, and, in horror, hauntings.

3. Because Josh is generally absent from the home and not helpful, Dalton tries to act as a fill-in for his father in aiding his mother.

4. The films do not make it clear what happened to Josh's father. His father's fate is another piece of information the audience is not made aware of, opening up the idea that

part of the reason why Josh struggles to be an active parent is due to an absence of a father figure growing up. This connects with Parker Crane's backstory in the sequel since, without a present father, his mother was able to inflict her full will upon him.

CHAPTER 5. MOTHER AS EXORCIST: *THE CONJURING* AND *THE CONJURING* 2

1. Ed and Lorraine Warren investigated many cases in their career, including Amityville. For insights into the many cases they were involved with, see Brittle.

2. The song is The Zombies' "Time of the Season" (1968). The lyrics after these are "Is he rich like me? / Has he taken, any time / To show you what you need to live?" The questioning of the father figure in the song connects with Roger's absence and struggle to provide for the family unit.

3. Dead Man's Bones is the artist behind the song, which was released in 2009. The sound is reminiscent of the time period that the film takes place in (1971). The chorus of the song and additional lyrics are like a warning from the house to the Warrens and Perrons about the spirits who also live in the house: "There's something in the shadows / In the corner of your room / A dark heart is beating / And waiting for you." The song breaks the fourth wall, in a way, by also communicating with the audience that it acknowledges what's happening.

4. Their appearance on the college campus was not simply for cinematic reasons. The Warrens did, in fact, host lectures about the occult primarily aimed at college students because of the renewed interest in the occult among younger audiences in the 1960s and '70s. As Brittle writes: "Amidst experimentation with alternate lifestyles, a sudden renewed interest in the occult sprang up. Closed for almost a century, the door to the 'underworld' was suddenly thrown open, followed by a drastic upswing in reported incidents of negative spirit phenomena. Almost immediately, the Warrens were inundated with what proved to be genuine cases of negative spirit oppression and possession" (10). Brittle adds: "Most of those affected at the time were persons of college age. Concerned about this grave development, the Warrens embarked on a program of campus lectures, wherein they warned students around the country about the dangers of the occult" (10).

5. The supposed reality of the Enfield case was far worse than the movie portrays. Brittle quotes an interview with Ed Warren:

"This Enfield case makes Amityville look like a playhouse," says Ed. "I mean that truly. The Lutzes were able to move out after twenty-eight *days* of terror; this is a case where the people can't move out for economic reasons, and have had to put up with the disturbances for three *years*. Those who are being victimized . . . are a divorced fifty-year-old woman and her three children who live together in a government-supported council house in the north London suburb of Enfield." (274–75, emphasis original)

Unlike in the movie, there was no question that the case was real and not a hoax. Ed recalled: "Even as I talked with the family, things would rise up in the air and float around the room. One evening a wooden chair lifted up in the air, stayed still for a moment, then exploded" (Brittle 276). The movie also differed from the real-life case in narrowing the haunting to only two spirits, when "it's as though there were six invisible people present" that talked to one another even when not being addressed by the people (Brittle 277).

6. The lyrics speculate on different ways the apocalypse could happen. Indeed, Janet's possession and the house's hauntings can be seen as apocalyptic events for the family. See Gelbart.

7. The government's inability to help Peggy and her family reflects the political climate of Britain at the time. In one scene, the television changes channels to a news broadcast where Queen Elizabeth II references the Iron Lady, the nickname given to Prime Minister Margaret Thatcher. Amongst Thatcher's conservative policies was cutting welfare-reform programs.

8. This is another point of exaggeration from the supposed real-life haunting. The Warrens began investigating supernatural phenomena in the 1940s and made sure to never investigate alone.

CHAPTER 6. TRAUMATIC MOTHERHOOD: *THE BABADOOK*

1. Just as Amelia avoids the trauma of Oskar's death, she also avoids the realities of her child. She has Claire babysit him while she goes to work. At work, she lies to her coworker Robbie and tells him that Samuel is home sick. Robbie covers for Amelia, but instead of going home, she goes to the mall where she sits on a bench and enjoys an ice cream. She escapes from reality into a place of distraction and entertainment, similar to the romantic movies she watches at night. For more information, see Buerger.

2. Samuel sits in the corner of the tree house while Ruby stands in front of him. He stands up and pushes her out of the tree house when she points out that he does not have a father. This scene highlights the cause of Samuel's anger and outbursts: his own trauma at not having a father in his life.

3. The ending can be read as Amelia being forced to confront her trauma. However, it can also be read as a continuation of her evasive behaviors in that she locks the monster in the basement and doesn't allow Sam down there, much like before, when it housed Oskar's belongings.

CHAPTER 7. THE DEVIL'S PROMISE: *THE WITCH*

1. Sam has a red blanket underneath him. Red is repeated throughout the film: the baby's blood that the witch smears on her body to regenerate, the witch's cloak when seducing Caleb, the blood in the goat's milk, the blood in the chicken egg, Caleb's blood as he bleeds from the temple, and finally, Katherine's blood on Thomasin's face and chest all feature red. The color is a sharp contrast to the bleak family farm and clothing.

2. In addition to being concerned about the welfare of his family, Caleb is fascinated with the state of his soul. He interrogates his father on their walk in the woods about whether Samuel's soul is in hell because he was not baptized. His death emphasizes this preoccupation in crying out for God's saving grace, having felt his soul had sinned through being seduced by the witch.

3. Norton writes:
Within a short period of time, the young women became the focal points around which all other members of the households revolved. That alone was extraordinary. Usually girls—whether daughters, nieces, or servants—resided at or near the bottom of the familial hierarchy. . . . But now others, including both male and female neighbors and familial superiors, were serving *them*. Most notably, the male heads of their

households and other adult men of their families gave them hours of concentrated attention, probably for the first time in their lives. (51)

4. Schiff, too, spends much of her work talking about gender-related issues.

5. For a great discussion on this topic in relation to the roles those from the Maine frontier played during the Salem witchcraft trials, see Norton. The film does not make it clear where the movie is supposed to take place in order to make it seem that it could take place anywhere in New England at the time.

CHAPTER 8. MATRILINEAL LEGACY: *HEREDITARY*

1. The film takes place in the Northwest and depicts a landscape that is mountainous and barren, much like something out of a painting or in a backdrop to an artwork.

2. As Annie later finds out, her mother was known and revered as "Queen Leigh" by the coven, a high priestess of Paimon. For more information on the significance of Paimon in demonology, see Crucchiola.

3. Peter is at least partially responsible for Charlie's death. He abandons her at the party in order to go upstairs and smoke weed. Before he does, he encourages her to eat a slice of the chocolate cake they give out. She does so without asking about nuts; as it turns out, it was laced with the allergen. Rather than call 911, Peter drives Charlie to the hospital himself. She rolls down a window to get air and is decapitated by a telephone pole. Peter's and Charlie's roles in her death underscore Paimon's description as a god of mischief who acts out if in female form.

CONCLUSION. MOTHERHOOD REVISITED

1. Douglas and Michaels acknowledge the roots of the term "momism" and how it continues to set the tone for derogatory views of motherhood:

The term "momism" was initially coined by the journalist Philip Wylie in his highly influential 1942 bestseller *Generation of Vipers*, and it was a very derogatory term. Drawing from Freud (who else?), Wylie attacked the mothers of America as being so smothering, overprotective, and invested in their kids, especially their sons, that they turned them into dysfunctional, sniveling weaklings, maternal slaves chained to the apron strings, unable to fight for their country or even stand on their own two feet. (4)

The authors explain that their work seeks "to reclaim this term, rip it from its misogynistic origins, and apply it to an ideology that has snowballed since the 1980s" (Douglas and Michaels 4).

2. One such film is *The Taking of Deborah Logan* (2014), which shows a daughter caring for her aging mother, who has Alzheimer's disease.

3. Peirce's adaptation opens with a flashback to Carrie's birth. Margaret attempts to kill her child to redeem herself of the sin of sex she and her husband took part in.

4. The original film (1983) has the resurrected Gage as a toddler-sized serial killer. In the remake, Ellie shows more awareness and understanding of her killing.

5. She believes her fetus urges her to kill those involved with her husband's death.

WORKS CITED

Aiello, Thomas. "*Rosemary's Baby* and Cold War Catholicism." *Unruly Catholics from Dante to Madonna: Faith, Heresy, and Politics in Cultural Studies*, edited by Marc DiPaolo, Scarecrow Press, 2013, pp. 111–24.

The Amityville Horror. Directed by Stuart Rosenberg, performances by James Brolin and Margot Kidder, Metro-Goldwyn-Mayer, 1979.

Aranjuez, Adolfo. "Monstrous Motherhood: Summoning the Abject in *The Babadook*." *Screen Education*, no. 92, Dec. 2018, pp. 122–28.

The Babadook. Directed by Jennifer Kent, performances by Essie Davis and Noah Wiseman, Umbrella Entertainment, 2014.

Bachelard, Gaston. *The Poetics of Space: The Classic Look at How We Experience Intimate Places*. Translated by Maria Jolas, Beacon Press, 1994.

Balanzategui, Jessica. "'The More You Deny Me, the Stronger I Get': 'Mister Babadook' and the Monstrous Empowerment of Children's Culture." Miller and Van Riper, pp. 107–19.

Beard, Drew. "Horror Movies at Home: Supernatural Horror, Delivery Systems and 1980s Satanic Panic." *Horror Studies*, vol. 6, no. 2, 2015, pp. 211–23. *MLA International Bibliography*, https://doi.org/10.1386/host.6.2.211_1.

Benson-Allot, Caetlin. "They're Coming to Get You . . . Or: Making America Anxious Again." *Film Quarterly*, vol. 72, no. 2, winter 2018, pp. 71–76. *MLA International Bibliography*, https://doi.org/10.1525/FQ.2018.72.2.71.

Benthien, Claudia. *Skin: On the Cultural Border between Self and the World*. Translated by Thomas Dunlap, Columbia UP, 2002.

Berenstein, Rhona. "Mommie Dearest: *Aliens*, *Rosemary's Baby*, and Mothering." *Journal of Popular Culture*, vol. 24, no. 2, 1990, pp. 55–73.

Briefel, Aviva. "Devil in the Details: The Uncanny History of *The Witch* (2015)." *Film and History*, vol. 49, no. 1, summer 2019, pp. 4–20.

Brittle, Gerald. *The Demonologist: The Extraordinary Life of Ed & Lorraine Warren*. Graymalkin Media, 2012.

Buerger, Shelley. "The Beak That Grips: Maternal Indifference, Ambivalence and the Abject in *The Babadook*." *Studies in Australasian Cinema*, vol. 11, no. 1, 2017, pp. 33–44.

Butler, Judith. *Gender Trouble: Feminism and the Subversion of Identity*. Routledge, 1990.

Caruth, Cathy. *Unclaimed Experience: Trauma, Narrative, and History*. John Hopkins UP, 1996.

Chang, Justin. "Film Review: *The Conjuring*." *Variety*, 22 June 2013, variety.com/2013/film/markets-festivals/film-review-the-conjuring-1200500864/.

Clover, Carol J. *Men, Women, and Chain Saws: Gender in the Modern Horror Film.* Princeton UP, 2015.

Cohen, Jeffrey Jerome. "Monster Culture (Seven Theses)." *Monster Theory: Reading Culture,* edited by Jeffrey Jerome Cohen, U of Minnesota P, 1996, pp. 3–25.

The Conjuring. Directed by James Wan, performances by Vera Farmiga and Patrick Wilson, Warner Bros. Pictures, 2013.

The Conjuring 2. Directed by James Wan, performances by Vera Farmiga and Patrick Wilson, Warner Bros. Pictures, 2016.

Creed, Barbara. *The Monstrous-Feminine: Film, Feminism, Psychoanalysis.* Routledge, 1993.

Crittenden, Jasmine. "Inner Dread: Psychology and Fate in *Hereditary.*" *Screen Education,* vol. 94, 2019, pp. 22–27.

Crofts, Penny. "Monstrous Bodily Excess in *The Exorcist* as a Supplement to Law's Accounts of Culpability." *Griffith Law Review,* vol. 24, no. 3, 2015, pp. 372–94. *Academic Search Premier,* https://doi.org/10.1080/10383441.2015.1134036.

Crucchiola, Jordan. "Explaining the Ending of *Hereditary.*" *Vulture,* 11 June 2018, vulture.com/article/hereditary-ending-explained.html.

Dead Man's Bones. "In the Room Where You Sleep." *Dead Man's Bones,* ANTI- Records, 2009. *Genius,* genius.com/Dead-mans-bones-in-the-room-where-you-sleep-lyrics.

Douglas, Susan, and Meredith Michaels. *The Mommy Myth: The Idealization of Motherhood and How It Has Undermined All Women.* Free Press, 2005.

The Exorcist. Directed by William Friedkin, performances by Linda Blair and Ellen Burstyn, Warner Bros. Pictures, 1973.

Fischer, Lucy. "Birth Traumas: Parturition and Horror in *Rosemary's Baby.*" Grant, pp. 439–58.

Freud, Sigmund. *The Uncanny.* Translated by David McLintock, Penguin Classics, 2003.

Friedan, Betty. *The Feminine Mystique.* W. W. Norton & Company, 1997.

Gelbart, Matthew. "A Cohesive Shambles: The Clash's 'London Calling' and the Normalization of Punk." *Music and Letters,* vol. 92, no. 2, May 2011, pp. 230–72.

Grant, Barry Keith, editor. *The Dread of Difference: Gender and the Horror Film.* 2nd ed., U of Texas P, 2015.

Hereditary. Directed by Ari Aster, performances by Toni Collete and Milly Shapiro, Lions Gate, 2018.

Hoffman, Robin A. "How to See the Horror: The Hostile Fetus in *Rosemary's Baby* and *Alien.*" *Lit: Literature Interpretation Theory,* vol. 22, no. 3, 2011, pp. 239–61.

Insidious. Directed by James Wan, performances by Patrick Wilson and Rose Byrne, Universal Pictures, 2011.

Johnson, Richard W, and Melissa M. Favreault. "Economic Status in Later Life among Women Who Raised Children Outside of Marriage." *Journal of Gerontology,* vol. 59B, no. 6, 2004, pp. S315–23.

Karlsen, Carol F. *The Devil in the Shape of a Woman: Witchcraft in Colonial New England.* W. W. Norton & Company, 1998.

Kord, T. S. *Little Horrors: How Cinema's Evil Children Play on Our Guilt.* McFarland, 2016.

Koresky, Michael. "Family Reunion." *Film Comment,* vol. 54, no. 3, May–June 2018, pp. 40–44. *ProQuest,* proquest.com/scholarly-journals/family-reunion/docview/2041706652/se-2.

Kristeva, Julia. *Powers of Horror: An Essay on Abjection.* Columbia UP, 1982.

Krzywinska, Tanya. "Demon Daddies: Gender, Ecstasy and Terror in the Possession Film." *Horror Film Reader,* edited by Alain Silver and James Ursini, Limelight Editions, 2000, pp. 247–68.

Maggi, Armando. "Christian Demonology in Contemporary American Popular Culture." *Social Research: An International Quarterly*, vol. 84, no. 4, winter 2014, pp. 769–93. *Business Source Premier*, https://doi.org/10.1353/sor.2014.0054.

Miller, Cynthia J., and A. Bowdoin Van Riper, editors. *Terrifying Texts: Essays on Books of Good and Evil in Horror Cinema*. McFarland, 2018.

Murphy, Bernice M. "'It's Not the House That's Haunted': Demons, Debt, and the Family in Peril Formula in Recent Horror Cinema." *Cinematic Ghosts: Haunting and Spectrality from Silent Cinema to the Digital Era*, edited by Murray Leeder, Bloomsbury Academic, 2015, pp. 235–52.

Musante, Dewey. "*Insidious* Forms: Deleuze, the Bodily Diagram and Haunted House Film." *Horror Studies*, vol. 7, no. 1, 2016, pp. 73–93. *MLA International Bibliography*, https://doi .org/10.1386/host.7.1.73_1.

Norton, Mary Beth. *In the Devil's Snare: The Salem Witchcraft Crisis of 1692*. Vintage Books, 2003.

Riede, Austin. "Bad Books and Fairy Tales: Stigmatized Guardians in Henry James's *The Turn of the Screw* and Jennifer Kent's *The Babadook*." Miller and Van Riper, pp. 132–44.

Risker, Paul. "Confronting Uncertainty: Jennifer Kent Discusses *The Babadook*." *Quarterly Review of Film and Video*, vol. 34, no. 1, 2017, pp. 13–17.

Rosemary's Baby. Directed by Roman Polanski, performances by Mia Farrow and John Cassavetes, William Castle Enterprises, 1968.

Scahill, Andrew. "Demons Are a Girl's Best Friend: Queering the Revolting Child in *The Exorcist*." *Red Feather Journal*, vol. 1, no. 1, 2010, pp. 39–55.

Schiff, Stacey. *The Witches: Suspicion, Betrayal, and Hysteria in 1692 Salem*. Back Bay Books, 2016.

Schoenherr, Richard A., and Lawrence A. Young. "Quitting the Clergy: Resignations in the Roman Catholic Priesthood." *Journal for the Scientific Study of Religion*, vol. 29, no. 4, 1990, pp. 463–81.

Shabot, Sara Cohen. "The Grotesque Body: Fleshing Out the Subject." *The Shock of the Other: Situating Alterities*, edited by Silke Horstkotte and Esther Peeren, Rodopi, 2007, pp. 57–67.

Sobchack, Vivian. "Bringing It All Back Home: Family Economy and Generic Exchange." Grant, pp. 171–91.

Stenzel, William. "It Would Be a Sin to Lose General Absolution." *U.S. Catholic*, vol. 68, no. 1, Jan. 2003, pp. 24–27.

Wessels, Emanuelle. "A Lesson Concerning Technology: The Affective Economies of Post-Economic Crisis Haunted House Horror in *The Conjuring* and *Insidious*." *Quarterly Review of Film and Video*, vol. 32, no. 6, 2015, pp. 511–26. *MLA International Bibliography*, https://doi.org/10.1080/10509208.2015.1034632.

Williams, Sara. "'The Power of Christ Compels You': Holy Water, Hysteria, and the Oedipal Psychodrama in *The Exorcist*." *Lit: Literature Interpretation Theory*, vol. 22, no. 3, 2011, pp. 218–38. *MLA International Bibliography*, https://doi.org/10.1080/10436928.2011.596385.

Williams, Tony. *Hearths of Darkness: The Family in the American Horror Film*. UP of Mississippi, 1996.

The Witch. Directed by Robert Eggers, performances by Anya Taylor-Joy and Kate Dickie, Pulse Films, 2016.

The Zombies. "The Time of the Season." *Odessey and Oracle*, CBS, 1968. *Genius*, genius.com/ The-zombies-the-time-of-the-season-lyrics.

INDEX

ABOUT THE AUTHOR

Lauren Rocha is assistant professor of practice of English and the first-year writing coordinator at Merrimack College. Her work has been published in such journals as *Journal of Gender Studies* and *Journal of International Women's Studies*. Her research interests are horror, gender, and popular culture.

Made in United States
North Haven, CT
17 March 2024

50017314R00118